Using Your Brain
—for a *CHANGE*

by
Richard Bandler

edited by
Steve Andreas
and
Connirae Andreas

Copyright © 1985
Real People Press
Box F
Moab, Utah 84532

ISBN: 0-911226-26-5 clothbound $10.00
ISBN: 0-911226-27-3 paperbound $6.50

Illustrations by Gustav Russ Youngreen

Library of Congress Cataloging in Publication Data

Bandler, Richard.
  Using your brain--for a change.

  Bibliography: p.
  Includes index.
  1. Neurolinguistic programming. I. Andreas, Steve.
II. Andreas, Connirae. III. Title.
BF637.N46B36 1985   158'.1'   85-10826
ISBN 0-911226-26-5
ISBN 0-911226-27-3 (pbk.)

Other books about Neuro-Linguistic Programming from Real People Press:

    FROGS INTO PRINCES, by *Richard Bandler and John Grinder.* 197 pp. 1979 Cloth $10.00 Paper $6.50

    REFRAMING: Neuro-Linguistic Programming and the Transformation of Meaning, by *Richard Bandler and John Grinder.* 220 pp. 1981 Cloth $10.00 Paper $6.50

    TRANCE-FORMATIONS: Neuro-Linguistic Programming and the Structure of Hypnosis, by *John Grinder and Richard Bandler.* 250 pp. 1981 Cloth $10.00 Paper $6.50

    The name *Real People Press* indicates our purpose; to publish ideas and ways that a person can use independently or with others to become more *real* —to further your own growth as a human being and to develop your relationships and communication with others.

2 3 4 5 6 7 8 9 10 Printing 90 89 88 87 86

Dedicated to
my mother

Contents

Most of us let our brains run wild, and spend a lot of time having experiences we don't want to have. Bandler pokes fun at many of our current ways of attempting to think about and solve human problems, as he begins to provide alternatives.

Depending upon the size, brightness, closeness, etc., of our internal pictures, we respond very differently to the same thoughts. Understanding these simple principles allows us to change our experiences so that we respond the way we want. "Briefest therapy" is demonstrated.

Seeing a memory from your own point of view (through your own eyes) has a very different impact than watching yourself in that memory from some other point of view. Knowing how to use this difference allows you to cure a phobia or a "post-traumatic stress syndrome" in a few minutes, among other things.

We often try to correct problems *after* something has gone wrong, rather than doing things ahead of time to make sure they go the way we want them to. The attempted correction often makes the problem worse.

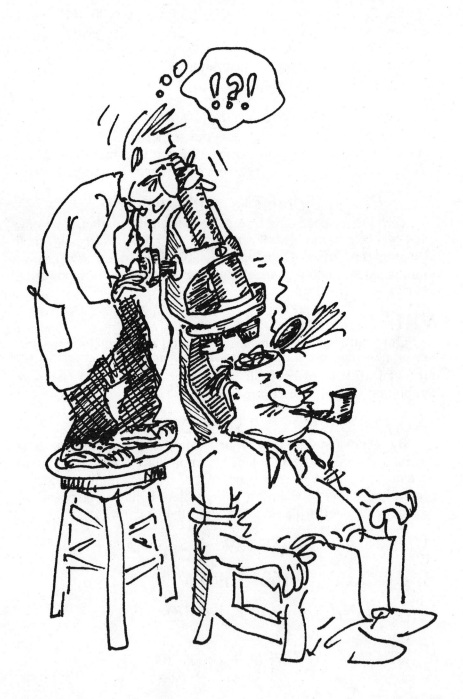

Introduction

How often have you heard the phrase, "She has a bright future" or, "He has a colorful past"? Expressions like these are more than metaphors. They are precise descriptions of the speaker's internal thinking, and these descriptions are the key to learning how to change your own experience in useful ways. For instance, right now notice how you picture a pleasant future event in your own life . . . and then brighten that picture and notice how your feelings change. When you brighten that picture, do you "look forward" to it more? Most people respond more strongly to a brighter picture; a few respond more to a dimmer picture.

Now take a pleasant memory from your past and literally make the colors stronger and more intense. . . . How does having a "colorful past" change the intensity of your response to that memory? If you don't notice a difference in your feelings when you make your memory more colorful, try seeing that memory in black and white. As the image loses its color, typically your response will be weaker.

Another common expression is, "Add a little sparkle to your life." Think of another pleasant experience, and literally sprinkle your image of it with little shining points of sparkling light, and notice how that affects your feeling response. (Television advertisers and designers of sequined clothing know about this one!)

"Put your past behind you," is common advice for unpleasant

1

events. Think of a memory that still makes you feel bad, and then notice *where* you see it now, and how far away the picture is. Probably it's fairly close in front of you. Now take that picture and physically move it far behind you. How does that change how you experience that memory?

These are a few very basic examples of the simplicity and power of the new NLP "Submodalities" patterns developed by Richard Bandler in the last few years. One of the earliest NLP patterns was the idea of "Modalities" or "Representational Systems." We think about any experience using sensory system representations—visual pictures, auditory sounds and kinesthetic feelings. Most NLP Training during the last ten years has taught a wide variety of rapid and practical ways to use this knowledge of modalities to change feelings and behavior. Submodalities are the smaller elements within each modality. For example, a few of the visual submodalities are brightness, color, size, distance, location, and focus. Knowledge of Submodalities opens up a whole new realm of change patterns that are even faster, easier, and more specific.

When we were first introduced to NLP in the fall of 1977, we set aside most of what we were doing in order to study these exciting and rapid new ways of changing behavior. At that time Richard Bandler and John Grinder were collaborating on the development of this new field, which promised a great deal. NLP taught how to follow a person's internal process by paying attention to unconscious eye movements, how to change old unpleasant feeling responses in minutes, and much more.

Now, seven years later, all those promises and *many* more have been kept. All the basic ideas and techniques of NLP have withstood the test of time, as well as the tougher test of teaching others how to make practical use of them. NLP has often been described as the field on the cutting edge of communication and change.

NLP offers a conceptual understanding that is solidly based on information science and computer programming, yet rooted even more thoroughly in the observation of living human experience. Everything in NLP can be directly verified in your own experience, or by observing others.

The new submodality patterns described and taught in this book are even faster and more powerful ways of creating personal change than the earlier NLP methods. There are only three major modalities, but there are *many* submodalities within each modality. Submodalities are literally the ways that our brains sort and code our experience. The submodality change patterns can be used to directly change the human software—the ways we think about and respond to our experiences.

Some critics have contended that NLP is too "cold" and "technical," and that while it may be successful with simple habits and phobias, it doesn't deal with "core existential issues." We will be interested in these critics' responses to the methods for changing understandings and beliefs demonstrated in chapters 6 and 7.

This book opens a doorway to a practical new way of understanding how your mind works. More important, this book teaches specific simple principles that you can use to "run your own brain." It teaches you how to change your own experience when you're not pleased with it, and to further enhance your enjoyment when your life is going well.

Many of us have the ability to take known principles and make useful adaptations of those principles, or make a small innovation now and then. Richard Bandler's special genius is his unparalleled ability to repeatedly delineate *new* principles, and to make them available to the rest of us. His sense of humor may sometimes sound caustic and arrogant, particularly when it is directed toward the professions of psychology and psychiatry (although other "experts" get their share!). This is at least partly understandable when you realize that although the NLP 10-minute phobia/trauma cure was first published over six years ago, most psychologists continue to believe that it takes months or years of talking and drugs (and several thousand dollars) to cure a phobia. We know well the frustration of being told, "It can't be done," when we have demonstrated it hundreds of times, *and* taught many others to do it consistently.

When a major technical innovation occurs in any industry, manufacturers around the world are eager to make immediate use of the new method, because they know that if they don't, competitors will put them out of business. Unfortunately, there is much more inertia in fields like psychology, in which professionals get paid *more* if they take longer to solve a problem. Since incompetence is rewarded, new and better methods take much longer to become part of the mainstream in these fields.

This inertia in the field of psychology has also been lamented by many others. Salvador Minuchin, well-known innovator in the field of family therapy, recently said:

> "How did people respond to our (research) findings? By defending their own paradigms. In response to new knowledge, there is always the question of how to maintain oneself doing the things one was trained in."

Despite this inertia, there are many exceptions within the fields of psychology and psychiatry—professionals who are eager to learn about any methods that can benefit their clients by making their work faster, better, and more thorough. We hope this book finds its way into your hands.

Several years ago we became aware of the new direction that Richard Bandler's genius was exploring, and we realized how useful these new patterns could be for people everywhere if they were more widely known. However, it is primarily our own personal fascination and excitement with submodalities that has led us to create this book.

Our raw materials were audiotapes and transcripts of a large number of seminars and workshops that Richard has taught recently. Then came a long process of sorting through and organizing this wealth of material, experimenting with it personally, and teaching it to others in order to gain a richer understanding. Finally, based on what we had learned, we have put this material together in the form of this book. We have tried to preserve the living style and flavor of the original seminars, while at the same time reorganizing and sequencing the material to make it easier to understand in written form.

Most books in rapidly developing fields are five or ten years out of date by the time they are printed. Most of the material in this book is about three years old. There are many other newer submodality patterns now being taught in advanced NLP seminars, and Richard continues to develop more patterns.

One of the basic principles of NLP is that the order or sequence of experiences, like the order of words in a sentence, affects their meaning. The order of the chapters in this book has been carefully thought out. Since much of the material in later chapters presupposes that you have the information and experiences presented in earlier chapters, you will have a much fuller understanding if you read them in order.

Another basic NLP principle is that words are only inadequate labels for experiences. It is one thing to read about hammering a nail into a board. It is quite a different experience to feel a hammer in your hand and hear a satisfying "thunk" as the nail sinks into a piece of soft pine. It is yet another experience to feel the vibration and twist in the hammer and watch the nail bend as you hear the "pinggg" that tells you about the hidden knot.

The patterns in this book are tools. Like any tools, they must be used to be understood fully, and they must be practiced to be used with consistent effectiveness. You can skim through this book rapidly if you just want to get an idea of what's in it. But if you really want to be able to use this information, be sure to try it out in your own experience and with others, or your knowledge will only be "academic."

Connirae Andreas
Steve Andreas
April 1985

I

Who's Driving the Bus?

Neuro-Linguistic Programming is a word that I made up to avoid having to be specialized in one field or another. In college I was one of those people who couldn't make up my mind, and I decided to continue that way. One of the things that NLP represents is a way of looking at human learning. Although lots of psychologists and social workers use NLP to do what they call "therapy," I think it's more appropriate to describe NLP as an educational process. Basically we're developing ways to teach people how to use their own brains.

Most people don't actively and deliberately use their own brains. Your brain is like a machine without an "off" switch. If you don't give it something to do, it just runs on and on until it gets bored. If you put someone in a sensory deprivation tank where there's no external experience, he'll start generating internal experience. If your brain is sitting around without anything to do, it's going to start doing *some*thing, and it doesn't seem to care what it is. *You* may care, but *it* doesn't.

For example, have you ever been just sitting around minding your own business, or sound asleep, when suddenly your brain flashes a picture that scares the pants off you? How often do people wake up in the middle of the night because they just relived an ecstatically pleasureable experience? If you've had a bad day, then later your brain will show you vivid reruns, over and over again. It's not enough that you had a bad day; you can

7

ruin the whole evening, and perhaps part of next week, too.

Most people don't stop there. How many of you think about unpleasant things that happened long ago? It's as if your brain is saying, "Let's do it again! We've got an hour before lunch, let's think about something that's really depressing. Maybe we can get angry about it three years too late." Have you heard about "unfinished business"? It's finished; you just didn't like the way it came out.

I want you to find out how you can learn to change your own experience, and get some control over what happens in your brain. Most people are prisoners of their own brains. It's as if they are chained to the last seat of the bus and someone else is driving. I want you to learn how to drive your own bus. If you don't give your brain a little direction, either it will just run randomly on its own, or other people will find ways to run it for you—and they may not always have your best interests in mind. Even if they do, they may get it wrong!

NLP is an opportunity to be able to study subjectivity —something that I was told in school is a terrible thing. I was told that true science looks at things objectively. However, I noticed that I seemed to be most influenced by my subjective experience, and I wanted to know something about how it worked, and how it affected other people. I'm going to play some mind-games with you in this seminar, because the brain is my favorite toy.

How many of you would like to have a "photographic memory"? And how many of you vividly remember past unpleasant experiences, over and over again? It certainly adds a little juice to life. If you go to see a terrifying movie, and you go home and sit down, the act of sitting down will tend to put you right back into the theater seat. How many of you have had that experience? And you claim that you don't have a photographic memory! You've already got one; you're just not using it in a directed way. If you're able to have a photographic memory when it comes to remembering past unpleasantness, it seems like it would be nice if you could deliberately harness some of that ability for more useful experiences.

How many of you have ever thought about something that

hadn't even happened yet, and felt bad about it ahead of time? Why wait? You may as well start feeling bad now, right? And then it didn't actually happen, after all. But you didn't miss out on that experience, did you?

That ability can also work the other way. Some of you have better vacations before you actually go, and then you get to be disappointed when you arrive. Disappointment requires adequate planning. Did you ever think about how much trouble you have to go to in order to be disappointed? You really have to plan thoroughly for it. The more planning, the more disappointment. Some people go to the movies and then say, "It's just not as good as I thought it was going to be." This makes me wonder, if they had such a good movie inside their heads, why did they go to the theater? Why go sit in a room with sticky floors and uncomfortable seats to watch a movie, and then say, "I can do better than that in my head, and I didn't even have the screen play."

This is the kind of thing that happens if you let your brain run wild. People spend more time learning how to use a food processor than they do learning how to use their brains. There isn't much emphasis placed on deliberately using your mind in ways other than you already do. You're supposed to "be yourself"—as if you had an alternative. You're stuck with it, believe me. I suppose they could wipe out all your memories with electroshock, and then make you into someone else, but the results I've seen haven't been very enticing. Until we find something like a mind-blanking machine, I think you're probably stuck with you. And it's not so bad, because you can learn to use your brain in more functional ways. That's what NLP is all about.

When I first started teaching, some people got the idea that NLP would help people program other people's minds to control them and make them less human. They seemed to have the idea that deliberately changing a person would somehow reduce that person's humanity. Most people are quite willing to change themselves deliberately with antibiotics and cosmetics, but behavior seems different. I've never understood how changing someone and making them happier turns them into less of a human being. But I *have* noticed how many people are very good at making their husbands or wives or children—or even total strangers—feel bad, just by "being themselves." I sometimes ask people, "Why be your *real* self when you can be something really worthwhile?" I want to introduce you to some of the infinite possibilities for learning and changing that are available to you if you start using your brain deliberately.

There was a time when film producers made movies in which computers were going to take over. People started thinking of computers not as tools, but as things that replaced people. But if you have seen home computers, you know that they have programs for things like balancing your checkbook! Balancing your checkbook on a home computer takes about six times as long as doing it the usual way. Not only do you have to write them in the checkbook, then you have to go home and type them into the computer. That's what turns home computers into planters —the things that you put flowers in. You play a certain number of games when it's a new toy, and after a while you stick it away in the closet. When friends come over whom you haven't seen for a long time, you pull it out so they can play the games you're bored with. That is not really what a computer is about. But the trivial ways people have used computers are much like the trivial ways in which people have used their own minds.

I keep hearing people say that you stop learning when you're about five, but I have no evidence that this is true. Stop and think about it. Between the ages of five and now, how many absolutely futile things have you learned, let alone worthwhile ones? Human beings have an amazing ability to learn. I am convinced, and I'm going to convince you—one way or the other—that you're still a learning machine. The good side of this is that you can learn things exquisitely and rapidly. The bad side is that you can learn garbage just as easily as you can learn useful things.

How many of you are haunted by thoughts? You say to yourself, "I wish I could get it out of my head." But isn't it amazing that you got it in there in the first place! Brains are really phenomenal. The things they'll get you to do are absolutely amazing. The problem with brains is not that they can't learn, as we have been told all too often. The problem with brains is that they learn things too quickly and too well. For example, think of a phobia. It's an amazing thing to be able to remember to get terrified every time you see a spider. You never find a phobic looking at a spider and saying, "Oh damn, I forgot to be afraid." Are there a few things you'd like to learn that thoroughly? When you think about it that way, having a phobia is a tremendous learning achievement. And if you go into the person's history, you often find that it was one-trial learning: it took only one instantaneous experience for that person to learn something so thoroughly that she'll remember it for the rest of her life.

How many of you have read about Pavlov and his dogs and the bell, and all that stuff? . . . and how many of you are salivating right now? They had to put the dog in a harness and ring the bell and give it food over and over again to teach it that response. All you did was *read* about it, and you have the same response the dog had. It's no big thing, but it is an indication of how rapidly your brain can learn. You can learn faster than any computer. What we need to know more about is the subjective experience of learning, so that you can direct your learning and have more control over your own experience and what you learn.

Are you familiar with the "our song" phenomenon? During a period of time when you were with someone very special, you had a favorite song you listened to a lot. Now whenever you hear that song, you think of that person and feel those good feelings again. It works just like Pavlov and salivation. Most people have no idea how easy it is to link experiences in that way, or how quickly you can make it happen if you do it systematically.

I once saw a therapist create an agoraphobic in one session. This therapist was a nice, well-intentioned man who liked his patients. He had years of clinical training, but he had no idea what he was doing. His client came in with a specific phobia of heights. The therapist told this guy to close his eyes and think about heights. Urrp—the guy flushes and starts to tremble. "Now think of something that would reassure you." Ummn. Now think about heights. Urrp. "Now think about comfortably driving your car." Ummn. "Now think about heights." Urrp. . . .

This guy ended up having phobic feelings about nearly everything in his life—what's often called agoraphobia. What the therapist did was brilliant, in a way. He changed his client's feelings by linking experiences. His choice of a feeling to generalize is not my idea of the best choice, however. He linked this man's feelings of panic to all the contexts that used to be reassuring in his life. You can use exactly the same process to take a good feeling and generalize it in the same way. If that therapist had understood the process he was using, he could have turned it around.

I've seen the same thing happen in couple therapy. The wife starts complaining about something the husband did, and the therapist says, "Look at your husband while you say that. You've got to have eye contact." That will connect all those bad feelings to the sight of her husband's face, so that every time she looks at him, she'll have those bad feelings.

Virginia Satir uses the same process in family therapy, but she turns it around. She asks a couple about special times in their early courting days, and when they start glowing, *then* she has them look at each other. She might say something like, "And I want you to realize that this is the same person you fell so deeply in love with ten years ago." That connects an entirely different feeling—generally a much more useful one—to the spouse's face.

One couple that came to see me had been in therapy with someone else for some time, but they still fought. They used to fight all the time at home, but when they came to me, they only fought in the therapist's office. The therapist probably said something like, "Now I want you to save all your fights for our sessions together so I can observe how you do it."

I wanted to find out if fighting was linked to the therapist or his office, so I had them experiment. I found out that if they went to the therapist's office when he wasn't there, they didn't argue, but if he held a session at their home, they did argue. So I just told them not to see that therapist any more. It was a simple solution that saved them a lot of money and trouble.

One client of mine couldn't get angry, because he would immediately get extremely scared. You could say he had a phobia of being angry. It turned out that when he was a child, any time he got mad, his parents got furious and scared him into the middle of next week, so those two feelings got linked together. He was grown and hadn't lived with his parents for fifteen years, but he still responded that way.

I came to the world of personal change from the world of mathematics and information science. Computer people typically don't want the things in their field to have anything to do with people. They refer to that as "getting your hands dirty." They like to work with shiny computers and wear white lab jackets. But I found out that there is no better representation of the way in which my mind works—especially in terms of limitations—than a computer. Trying to get a computer to do something—no matter how simple—is much like trying to get a person to do something.

Most of you have seen computer games. Even the simplest ones are quite difficult to program, because you have to use the very limited mechanisms the machine has for communication. When you instruct it to do something that it can do, your instruction has to be precisely organized in such a way that the information can be processed so that the computer can perform the task. Brains, like computers, are not "user-friendly." They do exactly what they're *told* to do, not what you *want* them to do. Then you get mad at them because they don't do what you *meant* to tell them to do!

One programming task is called modeling, which is what I do. The task of modeling is to get a computer to do something that a human can do. How do you get a machine to evaluate something, do a math problem, or turn a light on or off at the right time? Human beings can turn a light on and off, or do a math problem. Some do it well, others do it well sometimes, and some don't do it well at all. A modeler attempts to take the best representation for the way a person does a task, and make it available in a machine. I don't care if that representation really is how people do the task. Modelers don't have to have truth. All we have to have is something that works. We are the people who make cookbooks. We don't want to know *why* it is a chocolate cake, we want to know *what* to put in it to make it come out right. Knowing one recipe doesn't mean there aren't lots of other ways to do it. We want to know *how* to get from the ingredients to chocolate cake in a step-by-step fashion. We also want to know how to take chocolate cake and work backwards to the ingredients when someone doesn't want us to have the recipe.

Breaking down information in this way is the task of an information scientist. The most interesting information that you can learn about is the subjectivity of another human being. If somebody can do something, we want to model that behavior, and our models are of subjective experience. "What does she do inside her head that I can learn to do?" I can't instantly have her years of experience and the fine tuning which that produces, but I can very rapidly get some great information about the *structure* of what she does.

When I first started modeling, it seemed logical to find out what psychology had already learned about how people think. But when I looked into psychology, I discovered that the field consisted primarily of a huge number of descriptions about how people were broken. There were a few vague descriptions of what it meant to be a "whole person," or "actualized," or "integrated," but mostly there were descriptions about the various ways in which people were broken.

The current *Diagnostic and Statistical Manual III* used by psychiatrists and psychologists has over 450 pages of descriptions of how people can be broken, but not a single page describing health. Schizophrenia is a very prestigious way to be broken; catatonia is a very quiet way. Although hysterical paralysis was very popular during World War I, it's out of style now; you only find it occasionally in very poorly-educated immigrants who are out of touch with the times. You're lucky if you can find one now. I've only seen five in the past seven years, and two of them I made myself, using hypnosis. "Borderline" is a very popular way to be broken right now. That means you're not quite nuts, but not quite normal, either—as if anyone isn't! Back in the fifties, after *The Three Faces of Eve*, multiple personalities always had three. But since *Sybil*, who had seventeen personalities, we're seeing more multiples, and they all have *more* than three.

If you think I'm being hard on psychologists, just wait. You see, we people in the field of computer programming are so crazy that we can pick on anyone. Anybody who will sit in front of a computer for twenty-four hours a day, trying to reduce experience down to zeros and ones, is so far outside the world of normal human experience that I can say someone is crazy and still be worse.

Long ago I decided that since I couldn't find anyone who was as crazy as I was, people must not really be broken. What I've noticed since then is that *people work perfectly*. I may not like what they do, or they may not like it, but they are able to do it again and again, systematically. It's not that they're broken; they're just doing something different from what we, or they, want to have happen.

If you make really vivid images in your mind—especially if you can make them externally—you can learn how to be a civil engineer or a psychotic. One pays better than the other, but it's not as much fun. What people do has a structure, and if you can find out about that structure, you can figure out how to change it. You can also think of contexts where that structure would be a perfect one to have. Think of procrastination. What if you used that skill to put off feeling bad when someone insults you? "Oh, I know I ought to feel bad now, but I'll do it later." What if you delayed eating chocolate cake and ice cream forever—you just never quite got around to it.

However, most people don't think that way. The underlying basis of most psychology is "What's wrong?" After a psychologist has a name for what's wrong, then he wants to know *when* you broke and *what* broke you. Then he thinks he knows *why* you broke.

If you assume that someone is broken, then the next task is to figure out whether or not he can be fixed. Psychologists have never been very interested in *how* you broke, or *how you continue to maintain the state of being broken*.

Another difficulty with most psychology is that it studies broken people to find out how to fix them. That's like studying all the cars in a junkyard to figure out how to make cars run better. If you study lots of schizophrenics, you may learn how to do schizophrenia really well, but you won't learn about the things they *can't* do.

When I taught the staff of a mental hospital, I suggested that they study their schizophrenics only long enough to find out what they couldn't do. Then they should study normal people to find out how they do the same things, so they could teach that to the schizophrenics.

For example, one woman had the following problem: If she made up something in her mind, a few minutes later she couldn't distinguish that from a memory of something that had actually happened. When she saw a picture in her mind, she had no way of telling if it was something she had actually seen, or if it was something she had imagined. That confused her, and scared her worse than any horror movie. I suggested to her that when she made up pictures, she put a black border around them, so that when she remembered them later they'd be different from the others. She tried it, and it worked fine—except for the pictures she had made before I told her to do that. However, it was a good start. As soon as I told her exactly what to do, she could do it perfectly. Yet her file was about six inches thick with twelve years of psychologists' analyses and descriptions of how she was broken. They were looking for the "deep hidden inner meaning." They had taken too many poetry and literature classes. Change is a lot easier than that, if you know what to do.

Most psychologists think it's hard to communicate with crazy people. That's partly true, but it's also partly a result of what they do with crazy people. If someone is acting a little strange, he is taken off the streets, pumped full of tranquilizers and put in a locked barracks with thirty others. They observe him for 72 hours and say, "Gosh, he's acting weird." The rest of us wouldn't act weird, I suppose.

How many of you have read the article "Sane People in Insane Places"? A sociologist had some healthy, happy, graduate students admit themselves to mental hospitals as an experiment. They were all diagnosed as having severe problems. Most of them had a lot of trouble getting out again, because the staff thought their wanting to get out was a demonstration of their illness. Talk about a "Catch-22"! The patients recognized that these students weren't crazy, but the staff didn't.

Some years ago when I was looking around at different change methods, most people considered psychologists and psychiatrists to be experts on personal change. I thought many of them were much better demonstrations of psychosis and neurosis.

Have you ever seen an id? How about an infantile libidinal reaction-formation? Anybody who can talk like that has no business calling other people nuts.

Many psychologists think catatonics are really tough, because you can't get them to communicate with you. They just sit in the same position without even moving until someone moves them. It's actually very easy to get a catatonic to communicate with you. All you have to do is hit him on the hand with a hammer. When you lift the hammer to hit him again, he'll pull his hand away and say, "Don't do that to me!" That doesn't mean he's "cured," but he's now in a state where you can communicate with him. That's a start.

At one time I asked local psychiatrists to send me the weird clients they were having difficulties with. I found out that really weird clients are easier to work with, in the long run. I think it's easier to work with a flaming schizophrenic than it is to get a "normal" person to stop smoking when he doesn't want to. Psychotics seem to be unpredictable, and seem to flip in and out of their craziness unexpectedly. However, like anything else that people do, psychosis has a systematic structure. Even a schizophrenic doesn't wake up one day as a manic-depressive. If you learn how that structure works, you can flip him in and out. If you learn it well enough, you can even do it yourself. If you ever want to get a room in a full hotel, there's no better way than by having a psychotic episode. But you better be able to get back out of the episode again, or the room you get will be padded.

I've always thought that John Rosen's approach to psychosis was the most useful: enter the psychotic's reality and then spoil it for him. There are a lot of ways you can do this, and some of them aren't obvious. For instance, I had one guy who heard a voice coming out of electrical outlets, and the voice forced him to do things. I figured if I made his hallucinations real, he wouldn't be schizophrenic any more. So I hid a speaker in an outlet in my waiting room. When he came into the room, the outlet said "Hello." The guy turned around and looked at it and said, "You don't sound the same."

"I'm a new voice. Did you think there was only one?"

"Where did you come from?"

"Mind your own business."

That got him going. Since he had to obey the voice, I used that new voice to give him the instructions he needed to change what he was doing. Most people get a handle on reality and respond to it. When I get a handle on reality, I *twist* it! I don't believe that people are broken. They have just learned to do whatever they do. A lot of what people have learned to do is pretty amazing, and frankly I see more of that outside of mental hospitals than inside.

Most people's experience is not about reality, it's about *shared* reality. There are people who come to my door and give me religious comic books, and tell me the world is going to end in two weeks. They talk to angels, and they talk to God, but they're not considered crazy. But if a single person is caught talking to an angel, he is called crazy, taken to a mental hospital and stuffed full of drugs. When you make up a new reality, you'd better be sure that you get some friends to share it, or you may be in big trouble. That's one reason I teach NLP. I want to have at least a few others who share this reality, so the men in white coats don't take me away.

Physicists also have a shared reality. Other than that, there really isn't a lot of difference between being a physicist and being a schizophrenic. Physicists also talk about things you can't see. How many of you have seen an atom, let alone a sub-atomic particle? There is a difference: physicists are usually a little more tentative about their hallucinations, which they call "models" or "theories." When one of their hallucinations is challenged by new data, physicists are a tiny bit more willing to give up their old ideas.

Most of you learned a model of the atom that said there is a nucleus made up of protons and neutrons, with electrons flying around the outside like little planets. Niels Bohr got the Nobel prize for that description back in the 1920's. Over a period of about 50 years that model was the basis for an immense number of discoveries and inventions, such as the plastic in those naugahyde chairs you're sitting on.

Fairly recently, physicists decided that Bohr's description of the atom is wrong. I wondered if they were going to take back his Nobel prize, but then I found out Bohr is dead, and he already spent the money. The really amazing thing is that all the discoveries that were made by using a "wrong" model are still here. The Naugahyde chairs didn't disappear when physicists changed their minds. Physics is usually presented as a very "objective" science, but I notice that physics changes and the world stays the same, so there must be something subjective about physics.

Einstein was one of my childhood heroes. He reduced physics to what psychologists call "guided fantasy," but which Einstein referred to as a "thought experiment." He visualized what it would be like to ride on the end of a beam of light. And people say that he was academic and objective! One of the results of this particular thought experiment was his famous theory of relativity.

NLP differs only in that we deliberately make up lies, in order to try to understand the subjective experience of a human being. When you study subjectivity, there's no use trying to be objective. So let's get down to some subjective experience. . . .

II

Running Your Own Brain

I'd like you to try some very simple experiments, to teach you a little bit about how you can learn to run your own brain. *You will need this experience to understand the rest of this book, so I recommend that you actually do the following brief experiments.*

Think of a past experience that was very pleasant—perhaps one that you haven't thought about in a long time. Pause for a moment to go back to that memory, and be sure that you see what you saw at the time that pleasant event happened. You can close your eyes if that makes it easier to do. . . .

As you look at that pleasant memory, I want you to change the brightness of the image, and notice how your feelings change in response. First make it brighter and brighter. . . . Now make it dimmer and dimmer, until you can barely see it. . . . Now make it brighter again.

How does that change the way you feel? There are always exceptions, but for most of you, when you make the picture brighter, your feelings will become stronger. Increasing brightness usually increases the intensity of feelings, and decreasing brightness usually decreases the intensity of feelings.

How many of you ever thought about the possibility of intentionally varying the brightness of an internal image in order to feel different? Most of you just let your brain randomly show you any picture it wants, and you feel good or bad in response.

Now think of an unpleasant memory, something you think about that makes you feel bad. Now make the picture dimmer and dimmer. . . . If you turn the brightness down far enough, it won't bother you any more. You can save yourself thousands of dollars in psychotherapy bills.

I learned these things from people who did them already. One woman told me that she was happy all the time; she didn't let things get to her. I asked her how she did it, and she said "Well, those unpleasant thoughts come into my mind, but I just turn the brightness down."

Brightness is one of the "submodalities" of the visual modality. Submodalities are universal elements that can be used to change any visual image, no matter what the content is. The auditory and kinesthetic modalities also have submodalities, but for now we'll play with the visual submodalities.

Brightness is only one of many things you can vary. Before we go on to others, I want to talk about the exceptions to the impact brightness usually has. If you make a picture so bright that it washes out the details and becomes almost white, that will reduce, rather than increase, the intensity of your feelings. Usually the relationship doesn't hold at the upper extreme. For some people, the relationship is reversed in most contexts, so that increasing brightness decreases the intensity of their feelings.

Some exceptions are related to the content. If your pleasant picture is candlelight, or twilight, or sunset, part of its special charm is due to the dimness; if you brighten the image, your feelings may decrease. On the other hand, if you recalled a time when you were afraid in the dark, the fear may be due to not being able to see what's there. If you brighten that image and see that there's nothing there, your fear will decrease, rather than increase. So there are always exceptions, and when you examine them, the exceptions make sense, too. Whatever the relationship is, you can use that information to change your experience.

Now let's play with another submodality variable. Pick another pleasant memory and vary the size of the picture. First make it bigger and bigger, . . . and then smaller and smaller, noticing how your feelings change in response. . . .

The usual relationship is that a bigger picture intensifies your response, and a smaller picture diminishes it. Again there are exceptions, particularly at the upper end of the scale. When a picture gets very large, it may suddenly seem ridiculous or unreal. Your response may then change in *quality* instead of intensity —from pleasure to laughter, for instance.

If you change the size of an unpleasant picture, you will probably find that making it smaller also decreases your feelings. If making it really big makes it ridiculous and laughable, then you can also use that to feel better. Try it. Find out what works for you. . . .

It doesn't matter what the relationship is, as long as you find out how it works for *your* brain so that you can learn to control your experience. If you think about it, none of this should be at all surprising. People talk about a "dim future" or "bright prospects." "Everything looks black." "My mind went blank." "It's a small thing, but she blows it all out of proportion." When someone says something like that, it's not metaphorical; it's usually a literal and precise description of what that person is experiencing inside.

If someone is "blowing something out of proportion," you can tell her to shrink that picture down. If she sees a "dim future," have her brighten it up. It sounds simple, . . . and it is.

There are all these things inside your mind that you never thought of playing with. You don't want to go messing around with your head, right? Let other people do it instead. All the things that go on in your mind affect you, and they are all potentially within your control. The question is, "Who's going to run your brain?"

Next I want you to go on to experiment with varying other visual elements, to find out how you can consciously change them to affect your response. I want you to have a personal experiential understanding of how you can control your experience. If you actually pause and try changing the variables on the list below, you will have a solid basis for understanding the rest of this book. If you think you don't have the time, put this book down, go to the back of the bus, and read some comic books or the *National Enquirer* instead.

For those of you who really want to learn to run your own brain, take any experience and try changing each of the visual elements listed below. Do the same thing you did with brightness and size: try going in one direction . . . and then the other, to find out how it changes your experience. To really find out how your brain works, change only one element at a time. If you change two or more things at the same time, you won't know which one is affecting your experience, or how much. I recommend doing this with a pleasant experience.

1) *Color.* Vary the intensity of color from intense bright colors to black and white.

2) *Distance.* Change from very close to far away.

3) *Depth.* Vary the picture from a flat, two-dimensional photo to the full depth of three dimensions.

4) *Duration.* Vary from a quick, fleeting appearance to a persistent image that stays for some time.

5) *Clarity.* Change the picture from crystal-clear clarity of detail to fuzzy indistinctness.

6) *Contrast.* Adjust the difference between light and dark, from stark contrast to more continuous gradations of gray.

7) *Scope.* Vary from a bounded picture within a frame to a panoramic picture that continues around behind your head, so that if you turn your head, you can see more of it.

8) *Movement.* Change the picture from a still photo or slide to a movie.

9) *Speed.* Adjust the speed of the movie from very slow to very fast.

10) *Hue.* Change the color balance. Increase the intensity of reds and decrease the blues and greens, for example.

11) *Transparency.* Make the image transparent, so that you can see what's beneath the surface.

12) *Aspect Ratio.* Make a framed picture tall and narrow . . . and then short and wide.

13) *Orientation.* Tilt the top of that picture away from you . . . and then toward you.

14) *Foreground/background.* Vary the difference or separation between foreground (what interests you most) and background (the context that just happens to be there). . . . Then try reversing it, so the background becomes interesting foreground. (For more variables to try, see Appendix I)

Now most of you should have an experience of a few of the many ways you can change your experience by changing submodalities. Whenever you find an element that works really well, take a moment to figure out where and when you'd like to use it. For instance, pick a scary memory—even something from a movie. Take that picture and make it very large very suddenly. . . . That one's a thrill. If you have trouble getting going in the morning, try that instead of coffee!

I asked you to try these one at a time so that you could find out how they work. Once you know how they work, you can combine them to get even more intense changes. For example, pause and find an exquisitely pleasant sensual memory. First, make sure that it's a movie rather than just a still slide. Now take that image and pull it closer to you. As it comes closer, make it brighter and more colorful at the same time that you slow the movie to about half speed. Since you have already learned something about how *your* brain works, do whatever else works best to intensify that experience for you. Go ahead. . . .

Do you feel different? You can do that anytime . . . and you will have already paid for it. When you're just about to be really mean to someone you love, you could stop and do this. And with the look that's on your faces right now, who knows what you could get into . . . all kinds of fun trouble!

What's amazing to me is that some people do it exactly backwards. Think what your life would be like if you remembered all your good experiences as dim, distant, fuzzy, black and white snapshots, but recalled all your bad experiences in vividly colorful, close, panoramic, 3-D movies. That's a great way to get depressed and think that life isn't worth living. All of us have good and bad experiences; how we recall them is often what makes the difference.

I watched a woman at a party once. For three hours she had a great time—talking, dancing, showing off. Just as she was getting ready to leave, someone spilled coffee all down the front of her dress. As she cleaned herself up, she said, "Oh, now the whole evening is ruined!" Think about that: one bad moment was enough to ruin three hours of happiness! I wanted to find out how she did that, so I asked her about her dancing earlier. She said she saw herself dancing with a coffee-stain on her dress! She took that coffee-stain and literally stained all her earlier memories with it.

Many people do that. A man once said to me, "I thought I was really happy for a week. But then I looked back and thought about it, and realized that I wasn't really happy; it was all a mistake." When he looked backwards, he recoded all his experience and believed he had a rotten week. I wondered, "If he can revise his history that easily, *why* doesn't he do it the other way? Why not make all the unpleasant experiences nice?"

People often revise the past when they get divorced, or if they find out their spouse has had an affair. Suddenly all the good times they enjoyed together over the years look different. "It was all a sham." "I was just deluding myself."

People who go on diets often do the same thing. "Well, I thought that diet was really working. I lost five pounds a week for three months. But then I gained a pound, so I knew it wasn't working." Some people have successfully lost weight many times, but it never dawned on them that they were succeeding. One little indication that they're gaining weight and they decide, "The whole thing was wrong."

One man came to therapy because he was "afraid of marrying the wrong woman." He'd been with this woman and he thought he loved her, and really wanted to marry her, to the point where he'd pay to work on it in therapy. The reason he knew that he couldn't trust his ability to make this kind of decision is that he had married the "wrong woman" once before. When I heard him say that, I thought, "I guess when he got home from the wedding, he must have discovered that this was a strange woman. I guess he went to the wrong church or something." What on earth does it mean that he married the "wrong woman"?

When I asked him what it meant, I found that he had gotten a divorce after five years of marriage. In his case, the first four and a half years were really good. But then it got bad, so the whole five years were a total mistake. "I wasted five years of my life, and I don't want to do that again. So I'm going to waste the next five years trying to figure out if this is the right woman or not." He was really concerned about that. It wasn't a joke to him. It was important. But it never dawned on him that the entire question was inappropriate.

This man already knew that he and this woman made each other happy in many ways. He didn't think about asking himself how he was going to make sure he got even happier as he stayed with her, or how he was going to keep her happy. He had already decided that it was necessary to find out if this was the "right woman" or not. He never questioned his ability to make *that* decision, but he didn't trust his ability to decide whether to marry her or not!

Once I asked a man how he depressed himself and he said, "Well, like if I go out to my car and find there's a flat tire."

"Well, that is an annoyance, but it doesn't seem like enough to get depressed. How do you make that really depressing?"

"I say to myself, 'It's always like this,' and then I see a lot of pictures of all the other times that my car broke down."

I know that for every time his car didn't work, there were probably three hundred times that it worked perfectly. But he doesn't think of them at that moment. If I can get him to think of all those other times that his car worked fine, he won't be depressed.

Once a woman came to see me and told me that she was depressed. I asked her, "How do you know that you are depressed?" She looked at me and told me that her psychiatrist had told her. I said, "Well, maybe he's wrong; maybe you're not depressed; maybe this is happiness!" She looked back at me, raised one eyebrow, and said, "I don't think so." But she still hadn't answered my question: "How do you know that you're depressed?" "If you were happy, how would you know that you were happy?" "Have you ever been happy?"

I've discovered that most depressed people have actually had as many happy experiences as most other people, it's just that when they look back they don't think that it was really that happy. Instead of having rose-colored glasses, they have gray lenses. There was a marvelous lady up in Vancouver who actually had a blue hue over experiences that were unpleasant for her, but experiences that were pleasant had a pink hue. They were well sorted out. If she took one memory and changed the hue, it changed the memory totally. I can't tell you *why* that works, but that is *how* she does it subjectively.

The first time one of my clients said, "I'm depressed," I replied, "Hi, I'm Richard." He stopped and said, "No."

"I'm not?"

"Wait a minute. You're confused."

"I'm not confused. It's all perfectly clear to me."

"I've been depressed for sixteen years."

"That's amazing! You haven't slept in that long?"

The structure of what he's saying is this: "I've coded my experience such that I am living in the delusion that I have been in the same state of consciousness for sixteen years." I *know* he hasn't been depressed for sixteen years. He's got to take time out for lunch, and getting annoyed, and a few other things. Try to stay in the same state of consciousness for twenty minutes. People spend a lot of money and time learning to meditate in order to stay in the same state for an hour or two. If he were depressed for an hour straight, he wouldn't even be able to notice it, because the feeling would habituate and thereby become imperceptible. If you do anything long enough, you won't even be able to detect it. That's what habituation does, even with physical sensation. So

I always ask myself, "How is it possible for this guy to believe that he's been depressed all that time?" You can cure people of what they've got, and discover that they never had it. "Sixteen years of depression" could be only 25 hours of actually being depressed.

But if you take this man's statement, "I've been depressed for sixteen years," at face value, you're accepting the presupposition that he's been in one state of consciousness for that long. And if you accept the goal that you're going to go after making him happy, you'll be attempting to permanantly put him in *another* state of consciousness. You may in fact be able to get him to believe that he's happy all the time. You can teach him to recode everything in the past as happiness. No matter how miserable he is at the moment, he'll always appreciate that he's happy all the time. He'll be no better off, moment to moment—only when he looks into the past. You've just given him a new delusion to replace the one he walked in with.

A lot of people are depressed because they have good reason to be. A lot of people have dull, meaningless lives, and they're unhappy. Talking to a therapist won't change that, unless it results in the person living differently. If someone will spend $75 to see a psychiatrist, instead of spending it on a party, that's not mental illness, that's stupidity! If you don't *do* anything, then of course you're going to be bored and depressed. Catatonia is an extreme case of that.

When someone tells me she's depressed, I do the same thing I always do: I want to find out how to do it. I figure if I can go through it methodically step by step, and find out how she does it well enough that I can do it, then I can usually tell her something about how to do it differently, or else find somebody else who is not depressed and find out how that person does that.

Some people have an internal voice that sounds slow and depressed and makes long lists of their failures. You can talk yourself into very depressed states that way. It would be like having some of my college professors inside your head. No wonder those people are depressed. Sometimes the internal voice is so low that the person isn't consciously aware of it until you ask her. Because the voice is unconscious, she'll respond to it even more powerfully than if it were conscious—it will have a stronger hypnotic impact.

Any of you who have done therapy for a long time during a day may have noticed that there are times when you mentally drift away while you are seeing clients. Those are called trance states. If your client is talking about bad feelings and being depressed, you'll begin to respond to those suggestions, like anybody does in a trance. If you have "up" and cheerful clients, that can work for you. But if you have clients who are depressed, you can go home at the end of the day feeling terrible.

If you have a client who depresses herself with one of these voices, try increasing the volume of that voice until she can hear it clearly, so it won't have the hypnotic impact. Then change the tonality until it's a very cheerful voice. She'll feel a lot better, even if that cheerful voice is still reciting a list of failures.

Many people depress themselves with pictures, and there are a lot of variations. You can make collages of all the times things went wrong in the past, or you can make up thousands of pictures of how things *could* go wrong in the future. You can look at everything in the real world and superimpose an image of what it will look like in a hundred years. Have you heard the saying, "You begin dying the moment you're born." That's a great one.

Every time something nice happens, you can say to yourself, "This won't last," or "It's not real," or "He doesn't really mean it." There are many ways to do it. The question is always, "How does this person do it?" A detailed answer to that question will tell you everything you need to know in order to teach him how to do something else instead. The only reason that he doesn't do something more sensible is that it's all he knows how to do. Since he's done it for years, it's "normal"—unquestioned and unnoticed.

One of the wildest propensities in our culture is to act as if things are normal under any circumstances. The most elegant demonstration of that is New York City, as far as I'm concerned. If you walk down Broadway, no one's looking around and muttering "Good Lord!"

The next best demonstration is downtown Santa Cruz. People are doing things, right out on the street, that would put any mental hospital to shame. Yet there are men in business suits walking down the street talking to each other as if everything is completely normal.

I came from a "normal" environment, too. In my neighborhood, when I was nine years old and had nothing to do, I'd hang around with the guys. Somebody would say, "Hey, why don't we go out and steal a car?" "Let's go down and rob a liquor store, and murder someone."

I thought the way to succeed in life was to go live with the rich people. I thought if I hung around them, it would rub off. So I went to a place called Los Altos, where people have money. Los Altos Junior College at that time had sterling silver in the cafeteria, and real leather chairs in the student center. The parking lot looked like Detroit's current year showroom. Of course when I went there, I had to act like all that was normal, too. "Ho hum, everything's cool."

I got a job working with a machine that you communicate with, called a computer, and started as an information science student. They didn't have the department yet, because someone had stalled the funding for a couple of years. Since I was in school and there was no major there for me, I was lost in an existential crisis. "What will I do? I'll study psychology." About that time I got involved in editing a book about Gestalt Therapy, so I was sent to a Gestalt Therapy group to see what it was all about. This was my first experience of group psychotherapy. Everybody was crazy where I grew up, and everybody was crazy where I worked, but I expected people who went to therapists to be *really* crazy.

The first thing I saw there was somebody sitting and talking to an empty chair. I thought, "Oohhh! I was right. They *are* crazy." And then there was this other nut telling him what to say to the empty chair! Then I got worried, because everybody else in the room was looking at the empty chair, too, as if it were answering! The therapist asked, "And what does he say?" So I looked at the chair, too. Later I was told that it was a room full of psychotherapists, so it was OK.

Then the therapist said, "Are you aware of what your hand is doing?" When the guy said "No," I cracked up. "Are you aware of it now?" "Yes." "What is it doing? Exaggerate that movement." Strange, right? Then the therapist says "Put words to it." "I want to kill, kill." This guy turned out to be a neurosurgeon! The therapist said "Now, look at that chair, and tell me who you see." I looked, and there was still nobody there! But the guy looked over there and snarled, "My brother!"

"Tell him you're angry."

"I'm angry!"

"Say it louder."

"I'm *angry!*"

"About what?"

And then he starts telling this empty chair all these things that he's angry about, and then he attacks it. He smashes the chair to bits, and then apologizes, and works it out with the chair, and then he feels better. Then everyone in the group says nice things to him and hugs him.

Since I had been around scientists and murderers, I could act like everything was normal almost anywhere, but I was having trouble. Afterwards I asked the other people, "Was his brother really there?"

"Some of them said, "Of course he was."

"Where did you see him?"

"In my *mind's eye.*"

You can do just about *anything.* If you act as if it's normal, other people will too. Think about it. You can say "This is group psychotherapy," put chairs around in a circle, and say "This chair is the 'hot seat.' " Then if you say "Who wants to *work*?" everybody will start to get nervous while they wait. Finally someone who gets motivated when stress builds up to a certain point can't take it anymore: "I want to work!" So you say, "That chair's not a good enough place to do it. You come and sit in *this* special chair." Then you put an empty chair across from him. Often you'd start in the following way:

"Now, tell me what you're aware of."

"My heart is pounding."

"Close your eyes, and tell me what you're aware of."

"People are watching me."

Think about that for a minute. When his eyes are open, he knows what's going on inside; when his eyes are shut, he knows what's going on outside! For those of you who aren't familiar with Gestalt Therapy, this is a very common phenomenon.

There is a time and a place where people believed that talking to an empty chair was meaningful, and in fact it was. It can accomplish certain useful things. It was also very dangerous in ways they didn't understand, and many people still don't. People learn repeated *sequences* of behavior, and not necessarily the content. The sequence you learn in Gestalt Therapy is the following: When you feel sad or frustrated, you hallucinate old friends and relatives, become angry and violent, and then you feel better and other people are nice to you.

Take that sequence and translate it into the real world without the content. What does the person learn? When he's not feeling good, hallucinate, get angry and violent, and then feel good about it. How's that for a model for human relationships? Is that how you want to relate to your wife and children? But why take it out on a loved one? When you're furious, just go out and find a stranger. Walk up to him, hallucinate a dead relative, beat the snot out of him, and feel better. Some people actually do that, even without the benefit of Gestalt Therapy, but we don't usually think of that pattern of behavior as a cure. When people go through therapy, or any other repeated experience, they learn whatever's done really quickly, and they learn the pattern and sequence of what's done more that the content. Since most therapists focus on content, they usually won't even notice the sequence they're teaching.

Some people will look you straight in the eye and tell you the reason they are the way they are is because of something that happened long ago in their childhood. If that's true, they are really stuck, because of course then nothing can be done about it; you can't go have your childhood again.

However, the same people believe that you can pretend you are having your childhood again, and that you can go back and change it. The fact that you don't like what happened means that the event is "unfinished," so you can go back and "finish" it in a way that you like better. That's a *great* reframe, and it's a very useful one.

I think *everything* is unfinished in this sense: you can only maintain any memory, belief, understanding, or other mental process from one day to the next if you continue to do it. Therefore, it's still going on. If you have some understanding of the processes that continue to maintain it, you can change it whenever you don't like it.

It's actually quite easy to modify past experiences. The next thing I'd like to teach you is what I call "briefest therapy." One nice thing about it is that it's also secret therapy, so you can all try it now.

Think of an unpleasant embarrassment or disappointment, and take a good look at that movie to see if it still makes you feel bad now. If it doesn't, pick another one. . . .

Next, start that movie again, and as soon as it begins, put some nice loud circus music behind it. Listen to the circus music right through to the end of the movie. . . .

Now watch that original movie again. . . . Does that make you feel better? For most of you it will change a tragedy into a comedy, and lighten your feelings about it. If you have a memory that makes you annoyed and angry, put circus music with it. If you run it by with circus music, the next time it comes back it will automatically have the circus music with it, and it won't feel the same. For a few of you, circus music may be an inappropriate choice for that particular memory. If you didn't notice any change, or if your feelings changed in an unsatisfactory way, see if you can think of some other music or sounds that you think might impact that memory, and then try playing that music with your memory. You could try a thousand soap-opera violins, or opera music, the 1812 Overture, "Hernando's Hideaway," or whatever, and find out what happens. If you start experimenting, you can find lots of ways to change your experience.

Pick another bad memory. Run the movie however you usually do, to find out if it bothers you now. . . .

Now run that same memory backwards, from the end back to the beginning, just as if you were rewinding the film, and do it very quickly, in a few seconds. . . .

Now run the movie forward again. . . .

Do you feel the same about that memory after running it backwards? Definitely not. It's a little like saying a sentence backwards; the meaning changes. Try that on all your bad memories, and you'll save another thousand dollars worth of therapy. Believe me, when this stuff gets known, we're going to put traditional therapists out of business. They'll be out there with the people selling magic spells and powdered bat wings.

III

Points of View

People often say "You're not looking at it from my point of view," and sometimes they're literally correct. I'd like you to think of some argument you had with someone in which you were certain you were *right*. First just run a movie of that event the way you remember it. . . .

Now I want you to run a movie of exactly the same event, but from the point of view of looking over that other person's shoulder, so that you can see yourself as that argument takes place. Go through the same movie from beginning to end, watching from this viewpoint. . . .

Did that make any difference? It may not change much for some of you, especially if you already do it naturally. But for some of you it can make a huge difference. Are you still sure you were right?

Man: As soon as I saw my face and heard my tone of voice, I thought, "Who'd pay any attention to what that turkey is saying!"

Woman: When I was on the receiving end of what I'd said, I noticed a lot of flaws in my arguments. I noticed when I was just running on adrenalin and wasn't making any sense at all. I'm going to go back and apologize to that person.

Man: I really heard the other person for the first time, and what she said actually made sense.

Man: As I listened to myself I kept thinking, "Can't you say it some other way, so that you can get your point across?"

How many of you are as certain about being right as you were before trying this different point of view? . . . About three out of 60. So much for your chances of being right when you're certain you are—about 5%.

People have been talking about "points of view" for centuries. However, they've always thought of it as being metaphorical, rather than literal. They didn't know how to give someone specific instructions to change his point of view. What you just did is only one possibility out of thousands. You can literally view something from any point in space. You can view that same argument from the side as a neutral observer, so that you can see yourself and that other person equally well. You can view it from somewhere on the ceiling to get "above it all," or from a point on the floor for a "worm's eye" view. You can even take the point of view of a very small child, or of a very old person. That's getting a little more metaphorical, and less specific, but if it changes your experience in a useful way, you can't argue with it.

When something bad happens, some people say, "Well, in a hundred years, who'll know the difference?" For some of you, hearing this doesn't have an impact. You may just think, "He doesn't understand." But when some people say it or hear it, it actually changes their experience and helps them cope with problems. So of course I asked some of them what they did inside their minds as they said that sentence. One guy looked down at the solar system from a point out in space, watching the planets spin around in their orbits. From that point of view, he could barely see himself and his problems as a tiny speck on the surface of the earth. Other people's pictures are often somewhat different, but they are similar in that they see their problems as a very small part of the picture, and at a great distance, and time is speeded up—a hundred years compressed into a brief movie.

All around the world people are doing these great things inside their brains, and they really work. Not only that; they're even announcing what they're doing. If you take the time to ask them a few questions, you can discover all sorts of things you can do with your brain.

There is another fascinating phrase that has always stuck in my mind. When you're going through something unpleasant, people will often say, "Later, when you look back at this, you'll be able to laugh." There must be something that you do in your head in the meantime that makes an unpleasant experience funny later. How many people in here have something you can look back on and laugh at? . . . And do you all have a memory that you *can't* laugh at yet? . . . I want you to compare those two memories to find out how they're different. Do you see yourself in one, and not in the other? Is one a slide and one a movie? Is there a difference in color, size, brightness, or location? Find out what's different, and then try changing that unpleasant picture to make it like the one that you can already laugh at. If the one that you can laugh at is far away, make the other one far away too. If you see yourself in the one you laugh at, see yourself in the experience that is still unpleasant. My philosophy is: Why wait to feel better? Why not "look back and laugh" while you're going through it in the first place? If you go through something un-pleasant, you would think that once is more than enough. But oh no, your brain doesn't think that. It says "Oh, you fouled up. I'll torture you for three or four years. *Then* maybe I'll let you laugh."

Man: I see myself in the memory I can laugh about; I'm an observer. But I feel stuck in the memory I still feel bad about, just like it's happening again.

That's a common response. Is that true for many of the rest of you? Being able to observe yourself gives you a chance to "re-view" an event "from a different perspective" and see it in a new way, as if it's happening to someone else. The best kind of humor involves looking at yourself in a new way. The only thing that prevents you from doing that with an event right away is not realizing that you can do it. When you get good at it, you can even do it while the event is actually happening.

Woman: What I do is different, but it works really well. I focus in like a microscope until all I can see is a small part of the event magnified, filling the whole screen. In this case all I could see was these enormous lips pulsating and jiggling and flopping as he talked. It was so grotesque I cracked up.

That's certainly a different point of view. And it's also some-thing that you could easily try out when that bad experience is actually happening the first time.

Woman: I've done that. I'll be all stuck in some horrible situation and then I'll focus in on something and then laugh at how weird it is.

Now I want you all to think of two memories from your past: one pleasant and one unpleasant. Take a moment or two to reexperience those two memories in whatever way you naturally do. . . .

Next, I want you to notice whether you were *associated* or *dissociated* in each of those memories.

Associated means going back and reliving the experience, seeing it from your own eyes. You see exactly what you saw when you were actually there. You may see your hands in front of you, but you can't see your face unless you're looking in a mirror.

Dissociated means looking at the memory image from any point of view *other* than from your own eyes. You might see it as if you were looking down from an airplane, or you might see it as if you were someone else watching a movie of yourself in that situation, etc.

Now go back to each of those two memories, in turn, and find out whether you are associated or dissociated in each one. . . .

Whichever way you recalled those two memories naturally, I want you to go back and try experiencing them the *other* way, in order to discover how this changes your experience. If you were associated in a memory, step back out of your body and see that event dissociated. If you were dissociated, step into the picture or pull it around you until you are associated. Notice how this change in visual perspective changes your feeling experience of those memories. . . .

Does that make a difference? You bet it does. Is there anyone here who didn't notice a difference?

Man: I don't notice much difference.

OK. Try the following. Feel yourself sitting on a park bench at a carnival and see yourself in the front seat of a roller coaster. See your hair blowing in the wind as the roller coaster starts down that first big slope. . . .

Now compare that with what you would experience if you were actually sitting in the front seat, holding onto the front of the roller coaster, high in the air, actually looking down that slope. . . .

Are those two different? Check your pulse if you don't get more of a zing out of being *in* the roller coaster looking down the tracks. It's cheaper than coffee, too, for becoming alert.

Woman: In one of my memories it seems like I'm both in it and out of it.

OK. There are two possibilities. One is that you are switching back and forth quickly. If that's the case, just notice how it's different as you switch. You might have to slow down the switching a little in order to do that well.

The other possibility is that you were dissociated in the original experience. For instance, being self-critical usually presupposes a point of view other than your own. It's as if you're outside of yourself, observing and being critical of yourself. If that's the case, when you recall the experience and "see what you saw at the time" you'll also be dissociated. Does either of those descriptions fit your experience?

Woman: They both do. At the time I was self-critical, and I think I was flipping back and forth between observing myself and feeling criticized.

There is even a third possibility, but it's pretty rare. Some people create a dissociated picture of themselves while they are associated in the original experience. One guy had a full-length mirror that he carried around with him all the time. So if he walked into a room, he could simultaneously see himself walking into the room in his mirror. Another guy had a little T.V. monitor he'd put on a shelf or a wall nearby, so he could always see how he looked to other people.

When you recall a memory associated, you reexperience the original feeling response that you had at the time. When you recall a memory dissociated, you can see yourself having those original feelings in the picture, but without feeling them in your body.

You may, however, have a new feeling *about* the event as you watch yourself in it. This is what happens when Virginia Satir asks a question like, "How do you feel about feeling angry?" Try it. Recall a time when you were angry, and then ask that question,

"How do I feel *about* feeling angry?" In order to answer that question you have to pop out of the picture, and have a new feeling *about* the event as an observer rather than as a participant. It's a very effective way to change your response.

The ideal situation is to recall all your pleasant memories associated, so that you can easily enjoy all the positive feelings that go with them. When you are dissociated from your unpleasant memories, you still have all the visual information about what you may need to avoid or deal with in the future, but without the unpleasant feeling response. Why feel bad again? Wasn't it enough to feel bad once?

Many people do the reverse: they associate with, and immediately feel, all the unpleasantness that ever occurred to them, but their pleasant experiences are only dim, distant, dissociated images. And of course there are two other possibilities. Some people tend to always dissociate. These are the scientist/engineer types who are often described as "objective," "detached," or "distant." You can teach them how to associate when they want to, and regain some feeling connection with their experience. You can probably think of some times when this would be a real advantage for them. Making love is one of the things that's a *lot* more enjoyable if you're in your body feeling all those sensations, rather than watching yourself from the outside.

Others tend to always associate: they immediately have all the feelings of past experiences, good or bad. These are the people who are often described as "theatrical," "responsive," or "impulsive." Many of the problems they have can be cured by teaching them to dissociate at appropriate times. Dissociation can be used for pain control, for example. If you *watch* yourself have pain, you're not in your body to feel it.

You can do yourself a real favor by taking a little time to run through several of your unpleasant memories *dissociated*. Find out how far away you need to move the pictures so that you can still see them clearly enough to learn from them, while you watch comfortably. Then run through a series of pleasant experiences, taking time to associate with each one, and fully enjoy them. What you are teaching your brain to do is to *associate with pleasant memories,* and *dissociate from unpleasant ones.* Pretty soon your brain will get the idea, and do the same thing automatically with all your other memories.

Teaching someone how, and when, to associate or dissociate is one of the most profound and pervasive ways to change the quality of a person's experience, and the behavior that results from it. Dissociation is particularly useful for intensely unpleasant memories.

Does anybody in here have a phobia? I love phobias, but they're so easy to fix that we're running out of them. Look at that. The only people in here with phobias have phobias of raising their hands in an audience.

Joan: I have one.

Do you have a real, flaming phobia?

Joan: Well it's pretty bad. (She starts breathing rapidly and shaking.)

I can see that.

Joan: Do you want to know what it's about?

No, I don't. I'm a mathematician. I work purely with process. I can't know your inside experience anyway, so why talk about it? You don't have to talk about your inside experience to change it. In fact, if you talk about it, your therapist may end up being a professional companion. *You* know what you're phobic of. Is it something you see, or hear, or feel?

Joan: It's something I see.

OK. I'm going to ask you to do a few things that you can do in your mind really quickly, so that your phobia won't bother you at all, ever again. I'll give you the directions one part at a time, and then you go inside and do it. Nod when you're done.

First I want you to imagine that you're sitting in the middle of a movie theater, and up on the screen you can see a black-and-white snapshot in which you see yourself in a situation just *before* you had the phobic response. . . .

Then I want you to float out of your body up to the projection booth of the theater, where you can watch yourself watching yourself. From that position you'll be able to see yourself sitting in the middle of the theater, and also see yourself in the still picture up on the screen. . . .

Now I want you to turn that snapshot up on the screen into a black-and-white movie, and watch it from the beginning to just beyond the end of that unpleasant experience. When you get to the end I want you to stop it as a slide, and then jump *inside* the picture and run the movie backwards. All the people will walk backwards and everything else will happen in reverse, just like rewinding a movie, except you will be *inside* the movie. Run it backwards in color and take only about one or two seconds to do it. . . .

Now think about what it is you were phobic of. See what you would see if you were actually there. . . .

Joan: It doesn't bother me now, . . . but I'm afraid it may not work the next time I'm really there.

Can you find a real one around here so you could test it?

Joan: Yes, it's of elevators.

Great. Let's take a quick break. Go try it, and report back after the break. Those of you who are skeptical, go along and watch her, and ask her questions, if you want. . . . (For information about videotapes of the phobia cure, see Appendixes II, III, and IV.)

OK. How was it, Joan?

Joan: It's fine. You know, I'd never really seen the inside of an elevator before. This morning I couldn't even step into it, because I was too terrified, but just now I rode up and down several times.

That's a typical report. I almost got nervous one time, though. I was teaching in the Peachtree Plaza in Atlanta, which has a 70-story outdoor elevator. So I just had to find an elevator phobic. I cured this lady and sent her out of the seminar to test it. After about a half an hour I started thinking, "Oh oh, maybe she got up there and can't get down." When she came rolling in about fifteen minutes later, I asked her where she'd been. "Oh I was just riding up and down. It was really fun."

Once an accountant came to me with a phobia of public speaking that he'd been trying to get rid of for sixteen years. One of the first things he told me was that he had a total investment of over $70,000 in trying to cure his phobia. I asked him how he knew this, and he pulled out his therapy briefcase with all the cancelled checks in it. I said, "What about *your* time?" His eyes widened and he said, "I didn't figure that in!" He got paid about the same rate as a psychiatrist, so he had actually invested about $140,000 trying to change something that took me ten minutes to change.

If you can be terrified of an elevator, and then learn to respond differently, it seems like you should be able to change any pattern of behavior, because terror's a pretty strong behavior. Fear is an interesting thing. People move away from it. If you tell someone to look at something she's terrified of, she can't look at it. However, if you tell her to *see herself* looking at it, she's still looking at it, but for some reason she can do it that way. It's the same as the difference between sitting in the front seat of a roller coaster and sitting on a bench seeing yourself in a roller coaster. That is enough for people to be able to change their responses. You can use the same procedure with victims of rape, child abuse, and war experiences: "post-traumatic stress syndrome."

Years ago it took me an hour to work with a phobia. Then when we learned more about how a phobia works, we announced the ten-minute phobia cure. Now I've got it down to a few minutes. Most people have a hard time believing that we can cure a phobia that fast. That's really funny, because I *can't* do it slowly. I can cure a phobia in two minutes, but I can't do it in a month, because the brain doesn't work that way. The brain learns by having patterns go by rapidly. Imagine if I gave you one frame of a movie every day for five years. Would you get the plot? Of course not. You only get the meaning of the movie if all those pictures go by really fast. Trying to change slowly is like having a conversation one word a day.

Man: How about practice, then? When you create a change once, like with Joan, does she have to practice?

No. She's already changed, and she won't have to practice, or think about it consciously. If change work is hard, or takes much practice, then you're going about it in the wrong way, and you need to change what you're doing. When you find a path without resistance, you're combining resources, and doing it once is plenty. When Joan went into the elevator during the break, she didn't have to try not to be terrified. She was already changed, and that new response will last as well as the original terror.

One of the nice things about someone with a phobia is that she's already proved that she's a rapid learner. Phobics are people who can learn something utterly ridiculous very quickly. Most people tend to look at a phobia as a problem, rather than as an achievement. They never stop to think, "If she can learn to do that, then she should be able to learn to do anything."

It always amazed me that someone could learn to be terrified so consistently and dependably. Years ago I thought, "That's the kind of change I want to be able to make." That led me to wonder, "How could I *give* someone a phobia?" I figured that if I couldn't give someone a phobia, I couldn't be really methodical about taking it away.

If you accept the idea that phobias can only be bad, that possibility would never occur to you. You can make pleasant responses just as strong and dependable as phobias. There are things that people see and light up with happiness every single time—newborns, or very small children will do it for nearly everyone. If you don't believe it, I have a challenge for you: find the toughest, meanest-looking dude you can find, put a small baby in his arms and have him walk around inside a supermarket. You follow a couple of steps behind and watch how people respond.

I want to warn you about something, however: the phobia cure takes away feelings, and it will work for pleasant memories, too. If you use the same procedure on all your loving memories of being with someone, you can make that person into just as neutral an experience as an elevator! Couples often do this naturally when they get divorced. You can look at that person you once loved passionately, and have no feelings about her whatsoever. When you recall all the nice things that happened, you'll be watching yourself have fun, but all your nice feelings will be gone. If you do this when you're still married, you're really in trouble.

It's one thing to review all the experiences you have had with someone—pleasant and unpleasant—and decide that you want to end the relationship and move on. But if you dissociate from all the good times you had with that person, you'll be throwing away a very nourishing set of experiences. Even if you can't stand to be with her now, because you've changed or she's changed, you may as well enjoy your pleasant memories.

Some people go on to dissociate from all the pleasant experiences they're having now, "so they won't be hurt again later." If you do that, you won't be able to enjoy your own life even when it's nice. It will always be like watching someone else having fun, but you never get to play. If you do that with *all* your experiences, you'll become an existentialist—the ultimate totally uninvolved observer.

Some people see a technique work and decide to try it with everything. Just because a hammer works for nails doesn't mean everything needs to be pounded. The phobia procedure is effective in neutralizing strong feeling responses—positive or negative—so be careful what you use it for.

Do you want to know a good way to fall in love? Just associate with all your pleasant experiences with someone, and dissociate from all the unpleasant ones. It works really well. If you don't think about the unpleasant experiences at all, you can even use this method to fall in love with someone who does lots of things you don't like. The usual method is to fall in love this way and then get married. Once you're married, you can turn this process around so that you associate with the unpleasant experiences and dissociate from the pleasant ones. Now you respond only to the unpleasant things, and you wonder why "they've changed!" They didn't change, your *thinking* did.

Woman: Are there any other ways to do phobias? I'm scared silly of dogs.

There are *always* other ways to do things; it's a matter of "Do we know about them yet?" "Are they as dependable?" "How long do they take?" "What else will they affect?" and so on.

Try this: go back and recall a memory of something exquisitely pleasurable, exciting, and humorous from your past, and see what you saw at the time that it occurred. Can you find a memory like that? . . . (She starts to smile.) That's good. Turn the brightness up a little bit. . . . (She smiles more.) That's fine. Now keep that picture and have a dog come right through the middle of that picture and then become a part of that picture. As it does that, I want you to make the picture a little bit brighter. . . .

Now imagine being in the same room with a dog, to see if you're still phobic. . . .

Woman: I feel fine when I think of it now.

That procedure is a variation of another method I'll teach you later. It's not quite as dependable as dissociation for very strong phobias, but it will usually work. I've done a lot of phobias, so I'm bored with them, and I usually just do the fastest and most dependable thing I know. Now that you know it, you can do it, too. But if you really want to understand how brains work, the next time you have a phobic client, take a little longer. Ask a lot of questions to find out how this particular phobia works. For instance, sometimes a phobic person will make the picture of the dog, or whatever it is, very large, or bright, or colorful, or run a movie very slowly, or over and over again. Then you can try changing different things to find out how you can change this particular person's experience. When you get tired of that, you can always pull the quick cure out of your hip pocket and get rid of her in five minutes. If you do that kind of experimenting, you'll start learning how to *generate* NLP, and you won't have to pay to come to seminars any more.

IV
Going Wrong

I once asked a friend, "What is the biggest failure in your life?" He said, "In a couple of weeks I'm going to do this thing and it's not going to work out." You know what? He was right! It was the biggest failure of his life—not because it didn't work out, but because he took the time to feel bad about it *ahead of time*. Many people use their imagination only to discover all the things that would make them feel bad, so they can feel bad about it *now*. Why wait?

Why wait until your husband goes out and has an affair? Imagine it now; see him out there having fun with someone else. Feel as if you're there watching it all. You can make yourself hideously jealous, just like that. How many of you have done that?

Then if you're still feeling terrible when he comes home, you can yell and scream at him and drive him away, so that it will actually happen. Clients have come in and told me that they did this. I listen to them and I ask, "Why don't you make good pictures?" "What do you mean?" "Change that picture until you can see *yourself* there with him instead of that other woman. Then step into the picture and enjoy all those good feelings. Then when he gets home, make him want to do it with *you*." Do you like that better?

People often talk about having "good" and "bad" memories; but that's just a statement about whether they liked them or not.

51

Most people want to have only pleasant memories, and think they'd be much happier if all their bad memories went away. But imagine what your life would be like if you never had any bad experiences! What if you grew up and everything was wonderful all the time? You'd grow up to be a wimp, totally unable to cope; there are quite a few examples in this country.

Once I had a 24-year-old client who had been on valium since he was twelve. The only time he left his house was to go to the dentist, the doctor, or the psychiatrist. He'd been through five psychiatrists, but as far as I could tell, the major thing that was wrong with him was that he hadn't left his house in twelve years. *Now* his mother and father thought he should be out on his own. His father owned a big construction company, and complained to me, "That boy, it's time he got out on his own." I thought, "You turkey, you're twelve years too late. What are you going to do, give him your company so he can support you?" That company would have a life expectancy of about two days.

Since this kid had lived twelve years of his life on valium, he hadn't had many experiences—until they sent him to me! I made him go all kinds of places and do lots of weird things —either that or I'd beat the stuffing out of him. When he hesitated the first time and said he couldn't do something, I hit him really hard; that was the beginning of having experience. It was just an expedient way; I wouldn't recommend that you do this with most people. But there are times when a good rap on the side of the head constitutes the beginning of building a motivation strategy. Some of you may remember how that works from your younger years. I just put him in a lot of situations where he had to learn to cope with difficulties, and deal with other human beings. That gave him an experiential basis for living in the real world without the cushion of home, drugs, and a psychiatrist. The experiences I provided were a little more useful and relevant than talking to his psychiatrist about his childhood.

People say, "I can't do something" without realizing what those words mean. "Can't" in English is "can not" joined together. When somebody says, "I can't do it," he's saying he "can"—is able to—"not do it," which is always true. If you stop and pay attention, and listen to words, you begin to hear things that tell you what you can do.

I once worked with somebody who wanted to open a shyness and flirtation clinic. She brought me a bunch of people who were shy. I always thought shy people were shy because they thought about unpleasant things that would happen—like rejection, or being laughed at. I started asking these people my usual questions, "How do you know when to be shy? You're not shy all the time." Like all the things people do, shyness requires some process. It's no easy task. One man said, "I know it's time to be shy when I know that I'm going to meet somebody." "Well, what makes you shy?" "I don't think they'll like me." That statement is very different from "I think they won't like me." He literally said "I don't"—I do engage in the activity of not—"think they'll like me." He thinks anything *else* but that the person will like him. There were some people in the next room, so I said to him, "I want you to think that they'll like you." "OK." "Are you shy about meeting them?" "No." That seems a little too easy, but basically, *what works always turns out to be easy.*

Unfortunately in psychotherapy there isn't much incentive to find out what works quickly and easily. In most businesses, people get paid by succeeding at something. But in psychotherapy you get paid by the hour, whether anything is accomplished or not. If a therapist is incompetent, he gets paid *more* than someone who can achieve change quickly. Many therapists even have a rule against being effective. They think that influencing anyone directly is manipulative, and that manipulation is bad. It's as if they said, "You're paying me to influence you. But I'm not going to do it because it's not the right thing to do." When I saw clients, I always charged by the *change*, rather than by the hour; I only got paid when I got results. That seemed like more of a challenge.

The reasons that therapists use to justify their failures are really outrageous. Often they'll say, "He wasn't ready to change." That's a "jive excuse" if there ever was one. If he's "not ready," how can anyone justify seeing him week after week and charging him money? Tell him to go home, and to come back when he's "ready"! I always figured if somebody "wasn't ready to change," then it was my job to *make* him ready.

What if you took your car to a mechanic, and he worked on it for a couple of weeks, but it still didn't work. If he told you, "The car wasn't ready to change," you wouldn't buy that excuse would you? But therapists get away with it day after day.

The other standard excuse is that the client is "resistant." Imagine that your mechanic told you that your car was "resistant." "Your car just wasn't mature enough to accept the valve job. Bring it in again next week, and we'll try again." You wouldn't accept that excuse for a minute. Obviously the mechanic either doesn't know what he's doing, or the changes he's trying to make are irrelevant to the problem, or he's using the wrong tools. The same is true of therapeutic or educational change. Effective therapists and teachers can *make* people "ready to change," and when they're doing the right thing, there won't be any resistance.

Unfortunately, most humans have a perverse tendency. If they're doing something and it doesn't work, they'll usually do it louder, harder, longer, or more often. When a child doesn't understand, a parent will usually shout the exact same sentence, rather than try a new set of words. And when punishment doesn't change someone's behavior, the usual conclusion is that it wasn't enough, so we have to do it more.

I always thought that if something wasn't working, that might be an indication that it was time to *do something else!* If you know that something doesn't work, then *anything* else has a better chance of working than more of the same thing.

Non-professionals also have interesting excuses. I've been collecting them. People used to say, "I lost control over myself," or "I don't know what came over me." Probably a purple cloud or an old blanket did it, I guess. In the 60's people went to encounter groups and learned to say, "I can't help it; it's just the way I feel." If somebody says, "I just felt I had to throw a hand grenade into the room," that's not acceptable. But if someone says, "I just can't accept what you're saying; I have to yell at you and make you feel bad; it's just the way I feel," people will accept it.

The word "just" is a fascinating word; it's one of the ways to be *un*just to other people. "Just" is a handy way to disqualify everything but what you're talking about. If someone's feeling bad, and you say something nice to him, he'll often say, "You're *just* trying to cheer me up"—as if cheering someone up is a bad thing! It might be true that you're trying to cheer him up, but "just" makes it the *only* thing that's true. The word "just" discounts everything else about the situation.

The favorite excuse these days is, "I wasn't myself." You can get out of anything with that one. It's like multiple personality or the insanity defense. "I wasn't myself . . . I must have been *her!*"

All these excuses are ways of justifying and continuing unhappiness, instead of trying out something else that might make life more enjoyable and interesting for you—and for other people too.

Now I think it's time for a demonstration. Someone give me an example of something that you would expect to be a really unpleasant experience.

Jo: I always get anxious about confronting somebody. When someone's offended me in some way, and I want them to treat me differently, I confront them.

You expect that to be a negative experience?

Jo: Yes. And it isn't. It usually turns out to be much more positive. I may start out feeling uncomfortable, but I feel more comfortable as I get into it.

Does that make it useful?

Jo: It makes it a useful learning for me to actually confront them. Each time I do it, I get more confidence about confronting someone later on. It doesn't seem like I'm going to be confronting somebody, it seems more like I'm just going to be talking to them.

Well, think about it now. If you were going to confront someone, do you expect it to be unpleasant?

Jo: A little. Not as much as I used to.

I'm asking you to do it now.

Jo: Uhuh, a little bit.

You have to stop and take time to really do it. Think of someone whom it would be *very* hard to confront about something. Consider it, and find out how you can expect it to be unpleasant and succeed.

Jo: You would be difficult to confront.

I would be *lethal* to confront. What would propel you to have to confront someone?

Jo: If I felt like my integrity had been damaged—

"Damaged integrity." I had mine repaired.

Jo: Or if I'm insulted in some way. Sometimes when my ideas are being insulted—

Why do you have to confront someone?

Jo: I don't know.

What will happen if you do? What good does it do? Does it repair your integrity?

Jo: It makes me feel like I'm standing up for myself, protecting myself, preserving myself.

From . . . ? What I'm asking is, "What is the function of the behavior?" If you confront some people, they will kill you—even over a ham sandwich. I know that from where I grew up. Many people don't grow up in places like that, and if they're really lucky, they won't find out about it.

What is the significance of confronting someone? Does it have a function beyond giving you certain feelings which are different than the ones you have if someone "damages your integrity" by torturing your ideas? Do you *always* have to confront them? . . . Do you do it with everybody?

Jo: No.

How do you know who to go up to and confront, so that you can feel better?

Jo: People who I more or less trust, who aren't going to hurt me in some way.

That's a good choice. But you only confront them when they hurt you, or your ideas.

Jo: That's the only time that I confront them. There are lots of other times that I discuss things with them, but that's the only time that I'm confronting.

What makes it important enough to confront them? . . . Let me ask it another way. If they hurt your ideas, does that mean that they've misperceived them, or that they disagree with them?

Jo: Well, no. If they just misunderstand or disagree, that's all right. It's when someone says, "That's garbage" or something like that. It depends on the situation or the person.

Well, yes, it does depend on the situation, and that's very important. And I'm not saying confronting is not of value, either. I'm just asking, "How do you know when to do it?" and "How does this process work?" Would you go out and kill someone for damaging your integrity?

Jo: No.

There are a lot of people who would. Maybe it would be better if we taught them to do whatever you do. But I don't even know yet what it means for you to "confront" someone. I don't know if you yell and scream, or stick your finger up her nose, or cut her left ear off, or run her down with a truck. I'm making the assumption that your confronting is verbal.

Jo: It is.

I still don't know if your voice is at a high volume, or any other details. What's the difference between a "discussion" and a "confrontation?" How many of the rest of you thought you knew? . . . or didn't think about that? . . . or think I'm talking to her?

Jo: For me there's a lot of urgency around confronting somebody. I really want them to know how I feel about something. I really want them to know how I felt my ideas were received or rejected.

OK. What makes it urgent? What would happen if you didn't get them to understand? . . . Let me ask another question. Do they understand the idea and say bad things about it, or do they misunderstand and say bad things about it because they misunderstand? . . .

Jo: I appreciate what you're doing, I think you just gave me a different perspective. Have you?

I don't know. Give me a hint.

Jo: I think you did. Well . . . hmmm . . . it just seems different now. It doesn't seem like rejection any more; it just seems like they're trying to tell me something different. . . .

I don't know. I haven't even found out what it is we're working with here yet. You can't change yet, it's too soon. How could anything change that quickly, with just mere words, when I haven't even figured out what it is yet? . . . Does it matter?

Jo: No, but it changed. It changed.

It doesn't matter at all.

Jo: It doesn't matter to me what you said, or how you said it, or whether you knew what I was talking about. Something that you said just changed it. Somehow I don't feel like I'm going to have to confront any more.

Boy, have you got a surprise coming.

Jo: Well, I mean not confront anymore about the kind of thing I've been talking about.

Oh, there are other things that you confront about. Well, you could just do it randomly! That's what I do. Then you don't have to worry about whether it works or not.

Jo: Well, if I get overcharged for something, or get poor service or something, I'd confront.

Is that a way to continue to get good service in a restaurant?

Jo: It's a good way to get good service a lot of places.

Let me ask you another question. I'm not really picking on you. You're just a good focal point to get other people unconsciously. Did it ever occur to you to make people in a restaurant feel *so* good, *before* they served you, that they'd have no alternative but to give you good service . . . ?

Jo: I don't understand. . . . Somehow I lost that somewhere.

It always amazes me that people go to a restaurant to have a human being wait on them, and then don't treat him like one. Having been a waiter, I can tell you that most of the people who go to a restaurant treat you very strangely. There are a few people who come in and make you feel good, and that compels you to spend more time near them—regardless of whether they tip more or less. There is something about being around somebody who is nice to you that's more attractive than being around somebody who isn't nice—or who isn't even acknowledging that you exist.

Have any of you pretended with a child that he doesn't exist? Most kids will freak. Imagine being a waiter and having a room full of people doing that to you. Then someone treats you like you're not a machine, but a human being, and makes you feel good. Who would you hang around with more? One way to get good service in a restaurant is to treat the waiter well *first,* so as to make him *want* to treat you well.

The other alternative is to coerce him and make him feel bad enough to give you what you wanted, and expected to get without having to go through all the trouble of being nasty about it. If you do that, not only do you have to pay your bill, but you have to taint your own experience as well. Most people never think about that. Why should they go to a restaurant and be nice to a waiter? They should get good service automatically.

People often think of marriage in that way, too. "You should have known that." "I shouldn't have to tell him; he should do it automatically." And if he doesn't, that means it's time to get angry, intense, and force him to do it. And even when you win, what do you win? High self-esteem?

Man: An opportunity for your spouse to get even.

I've had a lot of people do that to me. I decided to take it up, and deliberately start getting even *ahead of time*! How many people have to get "even" when you do something nice to them? I'm not asking about whether you are nasty or nice; that's Santa's job. The question I'm asking you is, "Have you ever considered being considerate ahead of time?"

Woman: Yes, my strategy for a restaurant is to ask the waitress what she suggests is the best on the menu, and she'll pick out a selection. I look at that and suggest that she could make sure that it's fine, and the steak's not too small. I also ask her name, and talk to her by name.

So, yes, you've considered being nice, and actually attempted it. Like everything else in the world, it doesn't always work. But how many of you never even *considered* it when things weren't going well, or *before* things weren't going well? Why would a waiter go all the way down to a restaurant every night to give someone bad service, when they make their living by tips? Did you ever stop and consider that, Jo?

Jo: Yes, I did.

And you confronted them?

Jo: Well, I considered it, but I wasn't able to be as pleasant as I thought I should be. I wasn't able to be very agreeable when I was really disgusted. I wasn't able to change how I acted.

"She should have done it first anyway," right? Then you wouldn't have had to be disgusted, and had difficulty changing that.

Jo: Well, that's the way it seemed then. It seems very different now.

Now let's back up to the beginning. When we first started talking, Jo wanted to be more competent at being unpleasant. If you really heard what she was saying, it was, "I want to be able to stand up for myself and grumble and gripe more thoroughly." Nobody in the room heard her say that when she first talked. If they had heard it, they would have tried to teach her how to be more nasty. Think what an "assertiveness" trainer would have done with that! I have a new name for assertiveness training. I call it "loneliness preparation."

In contrast, *I ask questions to learn how to have someone else's limitations.* If I can learn how it works, then I can change it any way I want, and it will still work, but differently. You can't make a valid judgement about a process unless you know what it is, and you can't really know what it is unless you try it.

So I thought, "OK, Jo can't grumble and gripe. Where is it that she can't, because I want to learn how to not do it there?" I started asking her questions: "When do you do it?" "What is its purpose?" "Who do you do it with?" My questions go backwards in time. Starting with the problem, I backed up the process she goes through. When I backed her up far enough, she got to the place *before* she grumbled and griped, and *before* she even felt any inclination to do it. *That* is the place where she can go *around* it. If she takes the next step, the "problem" starts happening. But if she steps over to the side, she can go somewhere else that she likes better.

Jo goes into a restaurant, sits down, gets bad service, feels horrible, confronts the waitress, gets good service later and still feels bad. I asked, "Did it ever occur to you when you go into a restaurant and discover who your waitress is, to make her feel good?" She said, "I can't do that after I feel bad," and she's probably right. OK, why not do it right away all the time whenever you go into a restaurant, so you never get a chance to feel bad? That question directs her attention to an earlier time, when it's easy to do something different, and it also gives her something very specific to do differently.

Here's one you've all done. You come home feeling really

good. As you walk in the front door you see the living room is a mess, or someone forgot to take out the garbage, or you see that something else equally absolutely essential to your happiness is awry. You get angry inside, and frustrated; you suppress it and try to not feel angry and frustrated, but it doesn't work. So you go into therapy and you say, "I don't want to yell at my wife." "Why do you yell at your wife?" "Because I get frustrated and angry." Most clinicians will say, "Let it all out; express yourself; yell and scream at your wife." And to the wife they'll say, "Isn't it all right if he yells and screams at you? Can't you let him be himself?" You do your thing, and he'll do his . . . separately. That's nuts.

What most clinicians don't think about is that when he walks in the door and sees that mess, he *first* manages to get to the state where he's angry and frustrated, and *then* he tries to stop himself from getting angry and frustrated. The other thing they forget is what he's trying to accomplish by stopping himself from yelling at her in the first place: he's trying to get things to be pleasant. Well, why not go for it directly? Why not have the front door send him off into such pleasant thoughts about what he can do with his wife that he goes through the living room too fast to care about noticing anything else!

Whenever I say, "How about doing something *before* you feel so bad?" the client always looks stunned. It doesn't occur to him to back up. He always thinks that the only way he can make himself happy is to do what he wants exactly at the moment that he wants it. Is that the only way? It must be. The universe doesn't go backwards. Time won't go backwards. Light won't go backwards. But your mind *can* go backwards.

Typically clients will either not understand what I said at all, or will say, "I can't just do that!" It sounds too easy. So I found out I had to make them do it. They couldn't back up themselves, because they couldn't stop going where they were going. So I learned to ask them questions that would force them to go backwards. Often they fight me tooth and nail. They'll try to answer one question, and I insist that they answer another one to back them up another step.

When I get to the right point with a client, I ask a question that moves sideways and forward, and he goes forward again in the new direction. After that he can't stop going in the new direction. He's as stuck that way as the other, but he doesn't care because he likes being stuck that way. It works just like a spring: you compress it, and when you pull the lever over and release it, it flies forward again.

As soon as someone finds one of those places, he says, "Oh, I've changed. Let's go on now." It's so nonchalant. "How do you know you've changed?" "I don't know. It doesn't matter. It's different now." But Jo is still propelling forward on the new path. I've been testing her repeatedly. And she can't get back there to the other one now because it's too late.

I do this simply by presupposing that what is getting in her way is worth having, and all I need to do is find out where to use it. So, I take the behavior Jo is uncomfortable about—confronting—and take that back to before she even thinks about confronting. The same forces that used to drive her to confront and be uncomfortable about it will now compel her into another behavior.

What we have explored here with Jo is a common pattern in marriage. You want something from him, but he doesn't give it to you. So you feel bad. Then you tell him how bad you feel, hoping he'll be concerned enough to give it to you.

There are times when you don't get what you want from someone else. But when you don't get what you want, *feeling bad is extra!* Did you ever think of that? First you don't get what you want, and then you have to feel bad for a long time because you didn't get it. And then you have to feel bad to try to get it again. If you feel good, then you can just go back to that person and say, "Hey, you. Do you want to do this for me?" If you do that with a cheerful tone of voice, you're much more likely to get it, and without any future repercussions.

The greatest error of all is in thinking that the only way for you to feel good in certain situations is for someone else to behave in a certain way. "You must behave the way I want you to, so I can feel good, or I'm going to feel bad and stand around and make you feel bad too." When he is not there to behave in that way, then there's nobody to make you feel good. So you feel bad.

When he comes back, you say, "You were not here to have these behaviors to make me feel good, so I want you to feel bad now. I want you to be here *all the time.* No more bowling; don't go away for the weekend and go fishing; don't go to college; don't go to seminars; be here all the time. *I* can go away because I have a good time when I do, but when I come home you have to be here to make me feel good. If you love me you will do what I want, because when you don't do it, I feel bad, because I love you." Bizarre, huh? But that's how it works. And in a way, it's true. You sit there by yourself and you do feel bad. "If that person were here doing this, I'd feel good. What the hell's the matter with him?" Of course, if he's there and he's not willing to do it, that's even worse! People seldom stop and say, "Hey, what's going to be important to someone else?" It's even rarer that someone asks himself, "What could I do that would make her *want* to do this for me?"

If you feel inside you that when you don't get a certain amount of time from him, at the specified moment, then it's time to feel bad . . . and if you measure that bad feeling and you visualize him and connect that bad feeling with his face, then when he comes back and you see his face, you get to feel bad when he is there! That is amazing! Not only do you get to feel bad when he is *not* there; you also get to feel bad when he comes back! That doesn't sound like fun, does it? It's not fair to you to live that way.

And if he feels guilty about being gone, and he pictures what it will be like to come back to you, he will connect the feeling of guilt to the sight of your face. Then when he comes back and sees you, he will feel guilty again, and he won't want to be there either. These are the meta-patterns of obligation. They are both based on one tremendous error: the idea that marriage is a personal debt.

If you ask people what they want, they usually talk about wanting what they *don't* have, rather than what they already *do* have. They tend to ignore and take for granted what they already have and enjoy, and only notice what is missing.

Married people don't usually feel lucky, the way they did when they first met. Imagine what it would be like if every time you see him you feel *lucky*. And if he isn't there at a time when you want him—because he is doing something you wish he wouldn't do, because you don't want to do it with him—you still feel *lucky* that your special person is there for you much of the time. And when he's doing something else, you feel *lucky* that's the only price you have to pay. That isn't a heavy cost, is it? If you can't have that, then personally, I don't think it's worth it.

One thing that has always amazed me is that people are seldom nasty to strangers. You really have to know and love someone before you can treat her like dirt and really make her feel bad about small things. Few people will yell at a stranger about important things like crumbs on the breakfast table, but if you love her, it's OK.

One family came in to see me and the husband was really nasty. He pointed to his wife and snarled, "She thinks a 14-year-old girl should stay out until 9:30 at night!"

I looked him straight in the eye and said, "And *you* think that a 14-year-old girl should learn that men yell and scream at their wives, and make them feel bad!"

It's an awful thing to get lost.

Often a family will bring in a teenage daughter because there is something wrong with her; she enjoys sex and they can't get her to stop doing it. Talk about an idealistic, overwhelming, outrageous task: to get somebody to go back to being a virgin! The parents want you to convince their daughter that sex is not really pleasant, and that it is dangerous, and that if she enjoys it, it's going to influence her in a way that will make her feel bad for the rest of her life! Some therapists actually attempt that task, . . . and some even succeed.

One father literally dragged his daughter in to me with her arm twisted up behind her back, shoved her into a chair, and growled "Siddown!"

"Is anything wrong?" I asked.

"The girl's a little *whore!*"

"I don't need a whore; what did you bring her here for?"

That's an interruption if ever there was one! Those first lines are my favorites; you can really fry someone's brains with a line like that. Ask him one question after that, and he'll never be able to get back to where he was.

"No, no! That's not what I'm talking about—"

"Who is this girl?"

"My daughter."

"You made your daughter into a *whore*!!!"

"No, no! You don't understand—"

"And you brought her here to *me*! How disgusting!"

"No, no, no! You've got it all wrong."

This man who came in snarling and yelling, is now pleading with me to understand him. He has totally switched from attacking his daughter to defending himself. Meanwhile, his daughter has been quietly cracking up. She thought that was wonderful.

"Well, explain it to me then."

"I just think all these terrible things are going to happen to her."

"Well, if you teach her that profession, you're damn right!"

"No, no, you see it's—"

"Well, what is it you want me to do? What is it that you want?"

Then he started describing all the things he wanted. When he finished, I said, "You brought her in here with her arm twisted up behind her back and threw her around. That's how prostitutes are treated; that's what you're training her to do."

"Well, I want to force her to—"

"Oh, 'force'—teach her that men control women by throwing them around, ordering them around, twisting their arms behind their back, forcing them to do things against their will. That's what pimps do. Then the only thing left to do is to charge money for it."

"No, that's not what I'm doing. She's been sleeping with her boyfriend."

"Did she charge him?"

"No."

"Does she love him?"

"She's too young to love."

"Didn't she love you when she was a little girl?" . . . The image floats up from when she was a small child, sitting on daddy's knee. You can almost always get grumpy old men with that picture.

"Let me ask you something. Look at your daughter. . . . Don't you want her to be able to feel love, and to enjoy sexual behavior? The morals of the world have changed, and you don't have to like that. But how would you like it if the only way she learned to interact with men was the way you brought her in that door a few minutes ago? And she waited until she was twenty-five and married somebody who beat her up, threw her around, abused her, and forced her to do things against her will."

"But she may make a mistake, and it will hurt her."

"That's possible. Two years from now that guy may drop her like a hot rock and go away. And when she feels bad and lonely . . . she'll have no one to go to, because she'll hate your guts. If she came to you, you'd just say, 'I told you so.' "

"Even if she manages on her own in that time to go out and find somebody else and make a real relationship, when she has children of her own—*your grandchildren*—she'll never come and show them to you. Because she'll remember what you did, and she won't want her children to learn that. . . ."

Right now the father doesn't know what to think, so this is how you get him. You look him straight in the eye and say, "Isn't it more important that she learn to have loving relationships? . . . or should she learn to have the morals of any man that can force her around? That's what pimps do."

Try to get out of that one. There's no way out. There's no way his brain could go back now and do what he did before. He couldn't act like a pimp. It doesn't matter if you force somebody to *not* do something or to *do* something, or if you force her to do something "good" or something "bad." The way in which you force her teaches her to be controlled in that way.

The problem is, at that point he doesn't have anything else to do. He's stopped from doing what he used to do, but he doesn't have something else to do instead. I've got to give him something to do, like teach her the best way that's possible for a man to be with a woman. Because *then* if what his daughter has with this guy isn't good, she won't be satisfied with it. He was had then. You know what that means? He has to build a powerful positive relationship with his wife, and be nice to the other people in his family, and make his daughter feel good *more* with them than she does with this guy who's hanging around with her. How's that for a compulsion?

And I never once said, "How do you feel about that? What are you feeling now? What are you aware of?" or "Repent," or "Go inside and ask yourself."

People forget *so* easily what it is that they want. They go one step down the road to try to get it, and then get caught up in the way they're trying. They don't notice that the *way* they've chosen to get what they want doesn't work. When it doesn't work, they go to therapy to try to learn how to do it *better*. They haven't noticed that what they're trying to learn will give them exactly what they *don't* want.

When something happens that you don't like, you can always say, "It's your fault; I'm going to destroy you." That was probably pretty useful out in the jungle. But consciousness has got to evolve to the point where you say, "I've got a brain. Let's back up a little bit, keep in mind what I want, and go for it."

So every single time you feel bad about anything and you feel stuck, . . . or especially *right,* . . . or righteous, . . . I hope there is a little voice inside your head that says, "You're getting what you deserve!" And if you feel that there's nothing you can do about it, you're right—until you go inside your brain and back up, back up, back up, so you can move forward and go for it in another way.

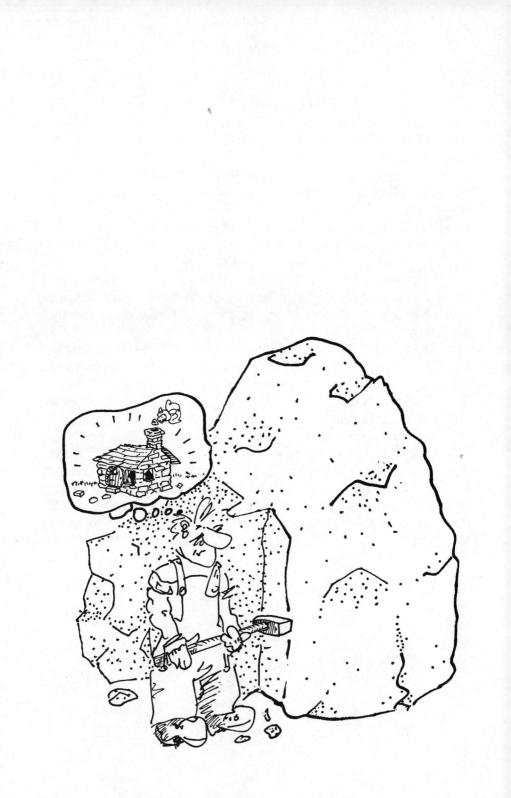

V

Going For It

In an attempt to understand why people do things, the field of psychotherapy has developed many models that they later found out simply weren't the case. However, many psychologists continue to hang on to them. We still have people who are looking for Ids and Egos, and they're as likely to find that as a "parent," a "child," or an "adult." I think that most psychologists must have watched too many horror movies when they were children. "You have a parent, an adult, and a child inside you that make you do things." It sounds like you need to be exorcised. People used to say, "The devil.made me do it." Now they say, "My parts made me do it."

"Well, you're just saying this because your 'parent' is talking.

"No I'm not; she's all the way back in New Jersey!"

Transactional Analysis is a device for separating behaviors into three parts—a little like multiple personality, except TA is supposed to be a cure. If you're really advanced, you get to have nine parts, because each of the first three parts has a parent, adult, and child inside of *them*! I never liked TA because only the child got to have any fun, and only the adult could be reasonable. Everyone has to have exactly the same parts, so there's no room for any individuality. TA is also a segregated society: my adult can't talk to your child, it can only talk to your adult. Why can't my child talk to your parent? It doesn't seem fair. But boy, can you convince people of that. How many of you bought that idea? Somebody explained it to you, and you thought, "Oh, yeah." Not everybody in the world has a parent, adult, and child that argue with each other. You won't find much of that in Tahiti. You have to go to a therapist to learn to have those problems.

How many of you have a "critical parent" voice inside you that berates you and tries to coerce you into doing things? If somebody suggests to you that there's a voice inside you that criticizes you all the time, and you start listening for it, guess what? You can install one. One interesting thing you can do is to agree with that critical voice, over and over again, until you drive it crazy. Another thing you can do is to change its location. Find out what happens if you hear that same voice coming out of your left big toe. . . . That change in location certainly changes the impact of that voice, doesn't it?

However, keep in mind that your critical voice could be right about what it's saying. Maybe you ought to listen to what it says, instead of just feeling bad. I'd like to show you what you can do with a critical voice that makes you feel bad; who has a nice loud one?

Fred: I've got one all the time.

Good. Can you hear it now?

Fred: Yes, it's criticizing me for speaking up.

Great. Ask if it will tell you *what it wants for you that is positive,* and listen to what it answers. Does that voice want you to be protected in some way? Does it want you to be more competent? There are many possibilities.

Fred: It wants me to succeed; it criticizes me when I stick my neck out.

OK, I assume that you agree with its intention. You want to succeed, too, right?

Fred: Yes. Sure.

Ask that voice if it believes it has good information that would be useful for you to have and understand. . . .

Fred: It says, "Of course."

Since it has good information, ask that voice if it would be willing to try changing the *way* it talks to you, if that would make it easier for you to listen and understand, so that you could succeed better. . . .

Fred: It's skeptical, but it's willing to try.

Good. Now, Fred, I want to ask you to think of ways that voice could be different, so that you would listen to it better. For instance, if it used a different voice tone that was soft and friendly, would you be more apt to pay close attention to it? Would it help if that voice gave you specific helpful instructions about what to do next, rather than criticize what you've already done?

Fred: I've thought of a couple of things it could do differently.

Good. Ask the voice if it would be willing to try those out, to find out if you actually do listen better if it talks to you differently. . . .

Fred: It's willing.

Tell it to go ahead and try it out. . . .

Fred: That's amazing. It's doing it, and it's not a "critical parent" any more. It's more like a friendly helper now. It's a pleasure to listen to it.

Sure. Who wants to listen to a voice that yells and criticizes? Real parents should try this technique too, when they want their kids to listen to them. If you use a nice tonality, children will listen to you. They may not agree with what you say, but at least they'll hear it. This procedure is something we've been calling "Reframing," and it's the basis for a set of negotiation skills that are useful in family therapy and business, as well as inside your own brain. If you want to learn more about it, read the book *Reframing.* The point I want to make here is that Fred's voice had forgotten its outcome until I reminded it. It wanted to motivate him to succeed, but all it was actually accomplishing was to make him feel bad.

While the women's liberation movement has had much positive impact, in some ways it has done the same thing. The original goal was to motivate people to change the way they think about and treat women. Women got educated about what kinds of behaviors are sexist. Now when someone *else* makes a sexist remark, *you* have to feel bad! It doesn't strike me as progress that now the "liberated" people have to feel bad when someone else uses a sexist word! What kind of liberation is that? That's just like being a kid, and when someone called you "stupid" or "ugly," it was time to feel bad and cry. People used to use sexist words and nobody noticed; now when they use those words, it's time to groan. Some liberation! Now you have a new set of reasons to feel bad. I used to go around to night clubs and pick out women who would react that way. "There's a good one. Watch this. I can make her feel terrible." "Hi chick." "Arrgghh!"

If you don't want people to use sexist language, it makes better sense to make *them* feel bad when they do it. That's a lot more fun, and a lot more effective, . . . and a lot more liberated, too.

One thing I like to do is go after women when they make sexist remarks.

A woman will say, "Well, the girls in the office—"

"How old are they?"

"Huh? They're in their 30's."

"You call them *girls*! They're *women*, you sexist pig! Do you call your husband a *boy*?"

If you do something to make people feel bad when they make sexist remarks, that at least puts the motivation to change where it belongs—in the person whose behavior you want to change. However, criticizing and attacking people really isn't the best way to get them to change. The best way is to discover how they already motivate themselves, and use that.

If you ask a lot of weird questions, and if you're persistent, you can find out how anyone does anything, including motivation. Many people are troubled by "lack of motivation," and one example of that is not being able to get up in the morning. If we study those people, we can find out how not to wake up, which could be of use to insomniacs. Everything that people can do is useful to someone, somewhere, sometime. But let's find out how someone wakes up easily and quickly, without drugs. Who in here regularly wakes up easily in the morning?

Betty: I get up easily.

OK. How do you get yourself up?

Betty: I just wake myself up.

I need a little more detail than that. How do you know when you are awake? What is the first thing that you are aware of when you are awake? Does the alarm wake you up, or do you just wake up, typically?

Betty: I don't have an alarm. I just realize that I'm not sleeping.

How do you realize that you are not sleeping? Do you begin to talk to yourself? Do you start to see something?

Betty: I tell myself.

What do you tell yourself?

Betty: "I'm awake. I'm waking up."

What allowed you to know that you could say that? The voice that says, "I'm waking up," is notifiying you that there is something to notice, so something must have preceded the voice. Was the voice commenting on a feeling, or was there suddenly light coming in? Something changed. Go back and remember it so that you can go through it sequentially.

Betty: I think it was a feeling.

What kind of a feeling? Warmth? Pressure?. . . .

Betty: Warm, yes.

Did you go from warmer to cooler, or from cooler to warmer?

Betty: The sensation of warmth became intensified. I felt my body get warmer.

As you began to become aware of warm feelings, you said to yourself, "I'm waking up." What happens right after that? You haven't seen anything yet? No internal images?

Betty: I said, "I have to get up."

Is the voice loud? Are there any other sounds, or is there just a voice in there? Does it have tone?

Betty: It is a very calm voice, it's an easy voice.

Does the tone of that voice inside change as you begin to wake up more and more?

Betty: Yes. It speeds up and becomes more clear and distinct, more alert.

This is an example of what we call a motivation strategy. It's not the whole thing, but it's enough to give us the key piece that makes it work to get her to do something. She has an internal voice that sounds like a sleepy, calm voice. Then as it says, "I have to get up," it begins to speed up and change that tone to one that is more awake and alert.

I want all the rest of you to try this. Doing it yourself is how you really find out about how other people do things. You don't have to say the same words, but take a moment to close your eyes, feel your body, and then listen to a voice inside your head. Have that voice begin to talk to you in a tone that is sleepy and calm. . . . Now have that voice speed up a little, become a little louder and more alert. Notice how your feelings change. . . .

Does that affect the way you feel? If it doesn't, check your pulse. An excited internal voice is a great way to wake yourself up whenever you need it. If you start talking to yourself and putting yourself to sleep at a time when you probably shouldn't, like on the freeway, you can learn to raise the volume and pitch, talk a little faster about something that is exciting, and it will wake you right up.

This is what many insomniacs do. They talk to themselves in a loud, high-pitched, excited voice, and it wakes them up—even if they're talking about how much they need to sleep. Insomniacs tend to be very alert and motivated. They think they don't sleep much, but studies have found that they actually sleep about as much as everybody else. What's different is that they also spend a lot of time *trying* to go to sleep, but they keep waking themselves up with their tone of voice.

The other main way to have insomnia is to look at lots of bright, flashing pictures. I asked one client what he did and he said, "Well, I start thinking about all the things that I may not be thinking about." I went home that night and tried it. "What is it I'm not thinking about?" Soon it was six in the morning, and I thought, "I know what it is—*sleep!*"

Now I want you to change your internal voice back the other way. Make it softer, lower, slower and sleepier, and notice how that makes you feel. . . .

Once I almost lost an audience doing this. Open your eyes and speed up that voice again, or you'll have to get the rest of this seminar unconsciously. This is something you can teach insomniacs, and it's also a process you can use yourself whenever you need it. For instance, I've learned that the best thing I can do on an airplane is to go unconscious. Between my house and the main airport is a short 20-minute flight. As soon as I sit down in the seat—sst—I'm out.

Man: When you're finding out how someone motivates herself, how do you know that you have gotten to the beginning of the sequence? For instance, Betty was saying the voice that was talking to her started getting louder. How do you know what questions to ask at that point?

That depends on your purpose in asking the questions. There is really no way to determine where somebody starts. You just need to get enough detail so that you can create the same experience. If I do it myself, and it works, then I've probably got enough information. The way to test these things is *in experience* —your own or someone else's.

Once I know someone's motivation strategy, I can literally motivate her to get out of a chair or do anything else by having her go through the same process: "Feel the chair, say to yourself, 'I have to get up.' Change your tonality and say it again in a voice that is faster, louder, and more alert." Whatever the process is that you use to get up in the morning, you probably use the same process to get yourself to walk downstairs to pick up a book, or to do anything else.

There are a lot of different ways that people use to motivate themselves. Rather than just tell you about them, I want you to get some experience of finding out about them on your own. Pair up with someone you don't know, and find out how she gets up out of bed in the morning. Everybody here had to do it at least this morning; the ones who can't do it didn't make it to this seminar. Start by asking simply, "How do you get up in the morning?" Your partner will give you one or two fairly general statements about what she does, and you'll have to ask more questions to get the rest of the details.

When you think you have the whole sequence, try it yourself to see if it works for you. For instance, your partner might say, "I see the light coming in through the windows, and I say to myself, 'get up' and I get up." If you try that yourself—you look at light in the windows and say to yourself "get up"—you don't necessarily get up. It's not quite enough. You have to do more than that to make it work. People do these things automatically and unconsciously, so often you have to ask a lot of questions in order to get all the pieces.

Since this isn't a strategies seminar, I don't insist that you get every little detail. But I do want you to get the basic pieces in the sequence, and get the key piece that makes a difference. That will usually be an element that *changes* in a crucial way. With Betty, it was a change in voice tone that actually got her up. To find that out, you really have to be a stickler for detail. If somebody says, "I make a picture of myself getting up," you have to ask for more detail. "Is it a movie? Is it a slide? Does it have color? Is it big? Do you say anything to yourself? What tone of voice do you use?" These small details are what make the sequence work. Some of them will be much more effective than others, and you can find that out by changing them one at a time, and noticing the impact. Pair up now and try this; take about fifteen minutes each. . . .

Well, what did you find in there? How does your partner motivate himself? What were the key pieces in the sequence?

Bill: My partner first hears the alarm clock, and he looks at it as he turns it off. Then he lies down again, and feels how comfortable he is in bed. An internal voice says, "If you stay here, you'll go to sleep and be late," and he makes a picture of a time when he was late to work, and feels bad. Then the voice says, "It will be worse next time," and he makes a bigger picture of what will happen if he's late again, and feels worse. The sequence seems to be "voice, picture, bad feeling." When the bad feeling is strong enough, he gets up.

That's what we call "the old anxiety routine." You keep generating unpleasant feelings until you're motivated to avoid them. Rollo May has that one. He even wrote a long book about it, which can be summarized in one sentence: "Anxiety has been *misunderstood*; anxiety is good because it gets people to do things." *If* your motivation strategy runs on anxiety, that's absolutely right. But not everyone has that kind of motivation. For other people anxiety *prevents* them from accomplishing things. They think of doing something interesting, then they make a picture of how things could go wrong, then they feel anxious and just sit at home.

Suzi: I do something very similar to what Bill's partner does. I tell myself that I can rest for a few more minutes, and I do. But as time passes, my picture of being late gets bigger and closer and brighter. It stays the same picture, but when it's big enough, I have to get out of bed to stop the bad feelings.

Do you procrastinate in other things? (Yes.) How many of the rest of you did term papers at the last minute? The longer you waited, the more motivated you were. Bill's partner has his own internal anxiety generator. Suzi's runs off the clock. They are both very similar in that they use unpleasant feelings as a motivator. Did any of you find an example of motivation that used pleasant feelings—even to do an unpleasant task?

Frank: Yes, Marge pictured all the things she was going to do during the day and felt good about doing them. She said that those pleasant pictures "pulled her out of bed."

What if she only had unpleasant things to do that day? Did you ask her about that?

Frank: Yes, I did. She said she made pictures of those things being all done, and felt wonderful that they were done. That good feeling pulled her out of bed, too. That seemed unreal to me. I can't imagine that actually working, and I wanted to ask you about it.

Where's Marge? . . . Marge, when do you do your taxes?

Marge: I have them done by mid-January. It's so nice to have them done, so I can do other things.

Well, it certainly seems to work for her. Nobody enjoys *doing* taxes, but most people enjoy having them *done*. The trick is to be able to access that good feeling of having them *done* ahead of time to get you started. Marge's motivation uses pleasant feelings instead of unpleasant ones. It's less common, and *very* strange to Frank, who does the opposite.

Lots of people are good at motivating themselves to do pleasant things. They just make pictures of *doing* the pleasant things, and are so attracted to these pictures that they start doing them. However, that process doesn't work for things you want to *have done*, but you don't like *doing* them. If you don't like doing taxes, and you make a picture of *doing* them, you'll feel repelled. That's not motivating at all. If you want to get motivated positively, you need to think about what's really attractive about a task. If you don't enjoy the task itself, what's attractive is *having it done*.

Actually there is another piece that needs to be there if Marge's motivation strategy is going to work. How many of you have thought about how nice it will be to have something done, and then you "ran out of gas" when you sat down and started on it?

Marge, when you start on your taxes, what keeps you going?

Marge: All along, I keep thinking about how nice it will be when they're all done.

That's an important piece, but I'll bet you also do something else.

Marge: Well, each time I write down a number or fill in a piece of the form, I feel good about getting that little piece done, too. It's like a little taste of the good feeling I'll have when it's *all* done.

Right. Those two pieces are what keep you going, and the second one will be more effective than the first. If you just think of it all being done, and it takes some time to finish a project, it can get to seem like "pie in the sky." But that good feeling of accomplishment you get every time you complete a small piece of the task will sustain you through a lot of drudgery.

Marge: That's interesting. It explains a lot of things in my life. People have often called me a "Pollyanna," because I'm always thinking of how good it will be when something unpleasant is over. I always get a lot done, but I've had trouble getting other people to do unpleasant jobs. When I tell them about how nice it will be when it's done, I usually get a blank stare.

Right. They just don't understand. That's not the way *they* motivate themselves.

Frank: It seems like you're saying that someone can be powerfully and effectively motivated without even having any unpleasant feelings. Is there any hope for the rest of us who propel ourselves with anxiety?

Sure. Like anything else people do, motivation strategies are learned, and you can always learn another one. It's fairly easy to teach you how to use Marge's strategy. But you have to be careful when you make such a pervasive change in someone's life.

Some people make lousy decisions, but since they aren't very motivated, they don't get into much trouble. If you teach them a really effective motivation strategy, they will actually carry out all those bad decisions, and do a lot of stupid, irrelevant, and possibly harmful things. So before I teach someone a powerful new motivation strategy, I make sure that the person already has an effective way of making decisions. If he doesn't, I'll teach him a new decision strategy *before* I teach him the new motivation strategy.

There are a lot of variations in how people motivate themselves, but we've already got examples of the two major patterns. Most people motivate themselves by thinking about how bad they will feel if they *don't* do something, and then they move *away* from that bad feeling. Rat psychologists call this "aversive conditioning."

A few people do the reverse, which is what Marge does. She uses pleasant feelings to move *toward* what she *does* want to have happen, instead of away from what she doesn't want to have happen—*and* she gets reinforcement along the way.

Someone with a motivation strategy like Marge's really lives in an entirely different world than most people—a world without a lot of the anxiety, unpleasantness, and stress that many people experience.

Many people have some combination of the two. They may first think of what will happen if they don't do something, and then think of how nice it will be when it's done.

All motivation strategies work, and you can't knock something that works. However, some of them are a lot faster and more tenacious, and a lot more enjoyable than others.

A lot of the problems that bring people into therapy, or into jail, have to do with motivation. Either they're not motivated to do things they want to do, or other people want them to do, or they *are* motivated to do things they, or other people, *don't* want them to do. What we've done here today is explore a little bit about how motivation works, so you can have some control over what you're motivated to do. What we've done here is only the beginning of what we can do with motivation, but it gives you something you can explore more on your own.

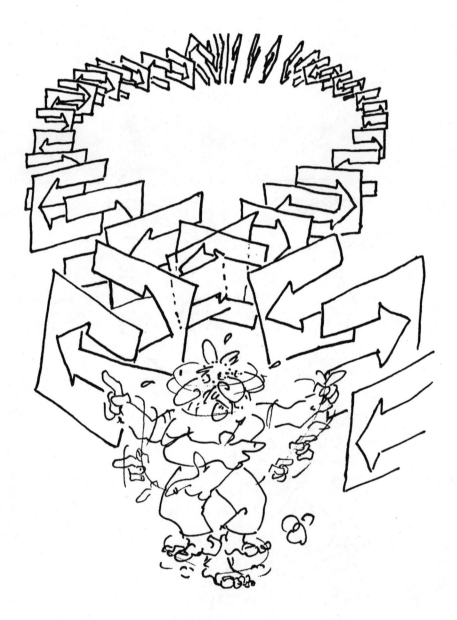

VI

Understanding Confusion

Many people get into difficulties because they're confused about something. I'd like to show you how to take confusion and make it into understanding. I need someone to play with, to demonstrate how this is done. After I demonstrate, I'm going to ask you to pair up and do it with each other, so pay attention.

Bill: I'd like to do that.

First think of something you're confused about, and you'd like to understand.

Bill: There are a lot of things I don't understand—

Stop. I want you to listen carefully to what I asked you to do. I did not ask you to think of something you don't understand; I asked you to think of something you're *confused* about. "Confusion" and "not understanding" are very different. There are a lot of things that you don't understand, because you don't know anything about them. You probably don't understand open-heart surgery or how to design a hydrogen bomb. You're not confused about them; you just don't have the information you'd need to understand how to do those things.

Confusion, however, is always an indication that you're on your way to understanding. Confusion presupposes that you have a lot of data, but it's not yet organized in a way that allows you to understand it. So I want you to think of something you're confused about: something you have a lot of experience with, but it doesn't make sense to you. . . .

83

Bill: OK. I'm thinking about—

Hold on. You're not allowed to tell me the content of what you're thinking about. You only need content if you are nosy. I'm a mathematician; I'm only interested in *form*. Besides it's too easy for the rest of these people to get lost in the content. I want them to learn the *process* that I'm demonstrating.

You've thought of something you're confused about. Now I want you to think of something similar that you understand. When I say similar, I mean that if your confusion is about someone's behavior, have your "understanding" also be about someone's behavior. If your confusion has to do with how a car engine works, make understanding be something mechanical, like how your toaster works, for example.

Bill: I've thought of something I understand.

Now you have two internal experiences; we're calling one of them "understanding" and the other one "confusion." Do they both have pictures?

Bill: Yes.

What I'm interested in are the *differences* between the two. How do they differ? For instance, one might be a movie and the other a slide. Or one might be in black and white and the other in color. I want you to go inside and examine those two experiences, and then tell me how they're *different*. . . .

Bill: Confusion is a slide, and it's small. Understanding is a movie, and it's large.

Are there any other differences? If the picture of confusion is smaller, it's probably also farther away.

Bill: Yes, it's farther away.

Do either of them have sound?

Bill: Yes, understanding has a voice describing what I see. Confusion is silent.

How do you know that you're confused about one, but you understand the other one?

Bill: I have different feelings when I look at those two pictures.

OK. How do your feelings know to feel that when you look at those pictures.

Bill: I suppose because I taught it that.

I want you all to notice something. I asked a "How?" question, asking about process, and he answered a "Why?" question. "Because" always answers "Why?" All you'll get out of "Because" is a bunch of historical theory. I only have one theory: that the reason people have so much trouble running their brains is because the Earth is tilted on its axis. So actually you have someone else's brain, and it's mad. That's as much theorizing as I do.

Let's try again. Bill, *how* do you know to have different feelings when you look at those two different pictures? . . .

Bill: I don't know.

I like that answer.

Bill: After I thought about it, I decided I didn't know.

That happens sometimes. Pretend you know. Talk. The worst thing that can happen is that you can be wrong. Years ago I realized I had been wrong so many times, I decided I'd just go ahead and be wrong in the ways that were more interesting.

Bill: When I look at the understanding picture, I can see how things work. That gives me a soft feeling of relaxation. When I look at the other one, I can't see what's going to happen next; I feel a little tense.

Those certainly sound like quite different experiences. Does anyone have any questions about what I've been doing?

Man: You make it look so easy. How do you know what questions to ask?

All I want to know is, "How are these two experiences different?" The answers to that are specific differences in the person's visual, auditory, and feeling experience. My questions are often directed at what the person is *not* noticing, and they are always directed toward helping that person make distinctions that he wasn't making before. For instance, when I asked Bill if it was a slide or a movie, he could answer easily. But he probably never even noticed that difference before, because no one ever asked him about it.

Woman: Is there any particular order to the questions you ask? You asked about whether it was a slide or a movie before you asked about color or black and white.

There's a certain efficiency in asking about things first and qualities later; you'll go astray less often. If you ask "How fast is it moving?" and it turns out to be a slide, that may be a little confusing to the person you're doing this with. Go for the basics first, and then ask about what other finer distinctions might be there.

The questions you ask are also a function of familiarity. I've explored confusion and understanding a few times before, so I already know what kinds of differences are likely to be there. It's like anything else you learn to do. When you do it the first time, you stumble around a bit. Later, when you're more familiar with what you're doing, you get more streamlined and systematic. You can also just make a long list of all the possibilities and go through them one by one. But it's easier if you first mention a few of the main distinctions to get that person's mind going in the right direction, and then ask, "How are the two different?"

Now let's go on to the more interesting part. Bill, I want you to take "confusion" and change it until it's the same as "understanding." I don't want you to change the content. I only want you to change the *process* that you use to represent the same content. First I want you to take that slide and make it into a movie. . . .

Bill: I can't seem to do that.

Do it this way. First make a series of slides at different times. When you have enough of them, look at them in rapid succession. Speed that up a little, and you'll have a movie. A movie is only a sequence of still pictures shown in a fast sequence.

Bill: OK. I've got a movie.

Good. Now add a narrative sound track that describes the movie. . . . (Bill nods.)

Now make that movie larger and closer until it's the same size and distance as your picture of understanding. . . . What happens when you do that? Do you understand it now?

Bill: Yes. I can see what's going on now; I feel much more comfortable. I have the same feeling with both pictures.

It makes sense that if you have a large movie with a narrative sound track, you'll understand something better than if all you have is a small, silent, still picture. You have much more information, and it's organized in a way that you can comprehend it. This is Bill's natural way of learning how to understand something.

Woman: Don't you have to have more information to get unconfused?

Sometimes that's the case. But often the person actually has the information; it just hasn't been accessed in a way that allows understanding. It's not that something is missing; it's just that what you have is poorly organized. You all know *much* more than you think you do. Usually it's not too little information that creates confusion, it's having too much information. Often a person's confusion is an enormous collage of data, or a lot of pictures flipping in rapid succession. In contrast, most people's pictures of understanding are well-organized, and very economical. They're like an elegant mathematical equation, or a good poem. They distill a lot of data down to a very simple representation. What I did with Bill just made it possible for him to collect the data that he already had, in a way that he could understand it. Being able to use your mind means being able to access, organize and use what you already have.

Most of you have seen what happens when a fire burns down in a fireplace. If you rearrange the logs a little bit, it will blaze up again. You haven't added anything. The only thing you've changed is the *arrangement,* but it makes a huge difference.

If you think that you need more data, you'll probably ask lots of questions. If the answers just contain raw data, they won't help you much, and you'll have to keep asking. The more answers you have, the less you will examine the questions you are asking. But if the answers help you *organize* the data you already have, it may help you to understand. That is what's often called "passive learning," someone who's always going, "Spoon-feed me." Other people can take in a large amount of data and organize it themselves without much help from outside. That's what's often called "active learning."

Now, Bill, I want you to try it the other way. Take what you originally understood and make it into a smaller, more distant, still picture and erase the sound track. . . .

Bill: Now I'm tense and confused.

So now we could take anything you're sure of, and confuse the hell out of you. You're all laughing; you don't realize how useful that can be! Don't you know someone who is sure they understand something, and they don't? . . . and that false confidence gets them into a lot of trouble? A good dose of confusion could get them motivated to listen to people around them and gather some very useful information. Confusion and understanding are internal experiences. They don't necessarily have anything to do with the outside world. In fact, if you look around, there usually isn't much connection.

In order for Bill to have the experience he calls "understanding," he has to go through a process in which the information he has is represented as a large movie with a sound track. This happens randomly sometimes, and at other times other people may induce it. However, now that he knows how it works, he can deliberately engage that process whenever he is confused about something. If he hasn't got enough data, he may not come to full understanding; his movie may have gaps in it, or the sound track may fade out from time to time. But it will be the best representation for him of what he knows. Those gaps in the movie will indicate precisely where he needs to have more information. And whenever he's bored with what he already understands too well, he can confuse himself as a prelude to coming to some new and different understanding.

Now I want you all to take turns doing what I did with Bill. Pair up with someone you don't know, because that will make it easier.

1) Ask your partner to think of a) something he is confused about, and b) something similar he understands. Your partner is not allowed to tell you anything about the content.

2) Ask,"How are these two experiences different?" You don't care about how they're similar, only how one is different from the other.

3) When you have at least two differences, ask your partner to change confusion to be the same as understanding.

4) Test what you've done by asking if he understands what was previously confusing. If he understands, you're done. If he doesn't understand, back up to step 2) and find some more differences. Keep going until either he understands, or he has identified what *specific* lack of information is preventing full understanding. Keep in mind that no one ever totally understands

anything. That's OK. It keeps life interesting. Take about fifteen minutes each. . . .

Most of you have probably noticed that your partner did something different inside than you do, in regard to the words "understanding" and "confusion." Let's first hear some of the differences you found, and then deal with any questions.

Man: My confusion is like a TV set with the vertical hold out of adjustment. The pictures keep rolling over so fast I can't see them. When I slowed it down and steadied it, it all made sense. But for my partner, confusion was a close panorama. So much was happening so close around her that she couldn't take it all in. She had to slow it down, and then physically back up and see it at a distance to understand it.

Man: My partner is a scientist. When he's confused, he just sees movies of things happening—what he calls "raw data." When he starts to understand, he sees little diagrams superimposed on the movies. These diagrams help him condense the events, and the movies get shorter and shorter until he gets what he calls a "moving still picture." It's a still picture with a superimposed diagram that indicates all the different ways that still picture can turn into a movie. That still picture sort of wiggles a little bit. It's very economical.

That's a great one. Do these make sense to the rest of you? We've got quite a variety already.

Woman: When I really understand something, I have five different clear pictures all at once, like a split-screen TV. When I'm confused I only have one picture, and it's fuzzy. But when my partner understands something it's always over here on her right side. Things she's confused about are in the center, and something she doesn't know anything about are over on her left.

Alan: What my partner did seemed very unusual to me. Her confusion was very focused and specific, and her understanding was a fuzzy, bright, movie that was out of focus. When she fuzzed up the confusion, she felt like she understood. I said to her, "Turn the knob, adjust the lens to get it out of focus."

You can do it that way, but you don't have to be metaphorical. People don't actually have knobs; you can just tell them to do it. So when she fuzzed it up, she understood. I hope she's not a heart surgeon! That's one of the strangest ones I've ever heard. If you blur the image, then you understand it! It certainly is different from the other ones we've gotten here. Did that seem odd to her, too?

Alan: Yes, it did. Could that be like turning it over to some lower-level unconscious process that you trust?

No, I don't accept explanations like that. *All* these processes are unconscious until you ask someone about them. There are many things we do intuitively, but this is different. Of course, you may have missed something important. But assuming that your description is correct, her understanding can't be connected with *doing* anything. In order to *do* something you have to have some specific detail. That's why I made that crack about hoping she wasn't a heart surgeon. With her kind of understanding, her patients wouldn't have a very high survival rate.

However, a fuzzy, bright understanding *will* be good for *some* things. For example, this is probably someone who would be lots of fun at a party. She'll be a very responsive person, because all she needs to do to feel like she understands what someone says is to fuzz up her pictures. It doesn't take a lot of information to be able to make a bright, fuzzy movie. She can do that really quickly, and then have a lot of feelings watching that bright movie.

Imagine what would happen if that woman married someone who had to have things crystal clear in order to understand. He'd say things like, "Now let's bring this into focus," and that would send her into confusion. When she described things she understood, they wouldn't be clear to him. If he complained that what she said was all fuzzy, she'd smile and be perfectly satisfied, but he'd be frustrated.

Her kind of understanding is the kind I talked about earlier, that doesn't have much to do with the outside world. It helps her feel better, but it won't be much help in coping with actual problems. It would be really useful for her to have another way of understanding—one that's more precise and specific.

In the last seminar I did there was a man whose "understanding" wasn't very useful for him. So he tried out the understanding process that his partner went through. Doing that gave him a totally new way of understanding that opened up a whole new world for him.

What I want you all to realize is that *all* of you are in the same position as that man, and the woman who fuzzes images. No matter how good you think your process of understanding is, there will always be times and places where another process would work much better for you. Earlier someone gave us the process a scientist used—economical little pictures with diagrams. That will work marvelously well for the physical world, but I'll predict that person has difficulties understanding people—a common problem for scientists. (Man: Yes, that's true.) People are a little too complex for a little diagram like that. Some other way of understanding will work better for people. The more ways you have of understanding, the more possibilities open up for you, and the more your abilities expand.

I'd like you all to try this experience of having someone else's understanding. Pair up with the same partner you had before. You already know something about that person's confusion and understanding, as well as your own. However, you do need to gather a little more information. You already found and listed the differences between your confusion and understanding, as well as your partner's. You haven't yet listed all the differences between your understanding and your partner's confusion. You'll have a lot of that information already, but you have probably missed some elements that were the same in what you compared earlier.

After you have full information about the difference between your understanding and your partner's confusion, pick any content that you understand, and first make it into your partner's confusion. Then make whatever changes are necessary to make it into their understanding. Your partner can give you directions and be a consultant to you, advising and answering any questions you may have. After you've tried out their understanding, compare your experience to your partner's, to see if they're the same. You may miss something on the first try, and have to go back and do it again. The goal is for you to *experience someone else's way of understanding*. After you try it out, you may decide it's not a very good one, and you may not want to use it very often. But don't be too sure about that; it may work exquisitely for something you have trouble with. At the very least it will help you to understand certain people who use that process. Take about twenty minutes each. . . .

Was that pretty interesting? What did you experience when you took on someone else's understanding?

Man: My own understanding is very detailed, so I understand mechanical things very easily. My partner's understanding was a lot more abstract: she sees fuzzy rainbows when she understands something. When I tried out her understanding I couldn't understand mechanical things at all, but I had a sense of understanding people much better. Actually, I think I wouldn't call it "understanding" so much as feeling what they meant and being able to respond to them easily. The colors were magnificent, and I felt sort of warm and excited the whole time. It certainly was different!

Woman: When I understand something, I just see detailed movies of that event happening. My partner sees two overlapping framed pictures when he understands something. The closer picture is an associated picture of the event, and the second picture is a dissociated picture of the same event. He feels he understands when the two pictures match. My partner's an actor, and I realized how useful it must be to him. When he's playing a part he's associated, *and* he also has the other dissociated picture that shows him what the audience is seeing at the same time. When I took on his understanding, I had a lot more information about how I look to other people. That was very helpful to me because I usually just jump into situations without thinking about how other people see me.

That sounds pretty useful. Taking on someone else's way of understanding is the ultimate way to enter that person's world. How many of you already had more or less the same way of understanding as your partner had? . . . About 8 out of 60. Here you just picked people at random. It's even more fascinating if you choose very successful people. I'm a pragmatist; I like to find out how really exceptional people do things. A very successful businessman in Oregon did the following with any project he wanted to understand: he'd start with a slide and expand it so that it was fully panoramic and he was inside it. Then he'd convert it into a movie. At any point where he had trouble seeing where the movie was going, he'd step back slightly and see himself in it. As soon as the movie started moving again, he'd step back inside. That's an example of a very practical understanding that is intimately related to actually doing something. For him, understanding something and being able to do it are indistinguishable.

Understanding is a process that is vital to survival and learning. If you weren't able to make sense out of your experience in some way, you'd be in big trouble. Each of us has about three pounds of gray matter that we use to try to understand the world. That three pounds of jelly can do some truly amazing things, but there's no way it can fully understand anything. When you think you understand something, that is always a definition of what you don't know. Karl Popper said it well: "Knowledge is a sophisticated statement of ignorance." There are several kinds of understanding, and some of them are a lot more useful than others.

One kind of understanding allows you to justify things, and gives you reasons for not being able to do anything different. "Things are this way because . . . and that's why we can't change anything." Where I grew up, we called that a "jive" excuse. A lot of "experts' " understanding of things like schizophrenia and learning disabilities is like that. It sounds very impressive, but basically it's a set of words that say, "Nothing can be done." Personally, I'm not interested in "understandings" that lead you to a dead end, even if they might be true. I'd rather leave it open.

A second kind of understanding simply allows you to have a good feeling: "Ahhh." That woman who defocuses pictures to get understanding is an example of that. It's sort of like salivating to a bell: it's a conditioned response, and all you get is that good feeling. That's the kind of thing that can lead to saying, "Oh, yes, 'ego' is that one up there on the chart. I've seen that before; yes, I understand." That kind of understanding also doesn't teach you to be able to do anything.

A third kind of understanding allows you to talk about things with important sounding concepts, and sometimes even equations. How many of you have an "understanding" about some behavior in yourself that you don't like, but that understanding hasn't helped you behave differently? That's an example of what I'm talking about. Concepts can be useful, but only if they have an experiential basis, and only if they allow you to do something different.

You can often get someone to accept an idea consciously, but only seldom will that lead to a change in behavior. If there's one thing that's been proved beyond a doubt by most of the religions of the world, that's it. Take "Thou shalt not kill," for instance. It doesn't say "except . . . " Nevertheless, the crusaders happily sliced Moslems in two, and the Moral Majority wants more missiles to wipe out a few more million Russians.

Often people in seminars will ask, "Is a visual person the same as the 'parent' in TA?" That tells me they are taking what I'm teaching and stuffing it into the concepts they already have. If you can make something new fit into what you already know, you will learn nothing from it, and nothing will change in your behavior. You will only have a comfortable feeling of understanding, a complacency that will keep you from learning anything new.

Often I'll demonstrate how to change a person in minutes, and someone will say, "Don't you think he was just fulfilling the expectations of the role situation?" I've rolled a few drunks, but I've never rolled a situation. Those are the people who come to seminars and get nothing for their money, because they leave with exactly the same understanding that they brought with them.

The only kind of understanding I'm interested in is the kind that allows you to *do* something. All our seminars teach specific techniques that allow you to do things. That seems simple. But sometimes the things I teach don't fit into your existing understanding. The healthiest thing you can do at that moment is to become confused, and many people complain about how confusing I am. They don't yet realize that *confusion is the doorway to a new understanding.* Confusion is an opportunity to rearrange experience and organize it in a different way than you normally would. That allows you to learn to do something new and to see and hear the world in a new way. Hopefully the last exercise gave you a concrete experience of how that works, and the kind of impact that can have.

If you understood everything I said, and never got confused, that would be a sure sign that you were learning nothing of significance, and wasting the money you paid to come here. That would be proof that you are continuing to understand the world in exactly the same way as when you got here. So whenever you get confused, you can get excited about the new understanding that awaits you. And you can be grateful for this opportunity to go somewhere new, even though you don't yet know where it will take you. If you don't like where it takes you, you can always leave. At the very least you will be enriched by knowing about it, and knowing that you don't like it.

Some people's understanding has uncertainty built into it. I know an engineer whose understanding is composed of a rectangular matrix of pictures, about eight rows down and eight columns across. He starts thinking he understands something when the matrix is about half full of pictures. When it's about ninety percent full, he knows he understands something pretty thoroughly. However, his matrix *always* has empty frames which signify that his understanding is always incomplete. That keeps him from ever getting too sure about anything.

One of my most capable student's understanding is a dissociated movie of herself doing whatever it is she understands. When she wants to actually do it, she steps into the movie—doing and understanding are nearly identical. Behind that movie is a succession of movies of herself doing it in different situations, doing it while overcoming obstacles, etc. The more different movies she has, the surer she is that she understands something well. I once asked her, "How many movies do you have to have to understand something?" She replied, "It's always a question of *how well* I understand it. If I have a few movies, that gives me a little understanding. If I have more movies, I understand better. The more different movies I have, the more I understand it. But I never understand completely."

In contrast, there are people who are completely confident that they understand how to do something if they have a single movie of having done it. I know one man who flew a plane once, so he was completely sure that he could fly any plane, anywhere, anytime, in any weather, while standing up in a hammock! He came to a five-day seminar of mine, learned one pattern and left at noon the first day, totally confident that he knew all of NLP. How's that for getting stuck?

Getting stuck in a particular way of understanding the world—whatever it is—is the cause of three major human diseases that I'd like to do something about. The first one is seriousness, as in "dead serious." If you decide that you want to do something, fine, but getting serious about it will only blind you and get in your way.

Being right, or certain, is the second disease. Certainty is where people stop thinking and stop noticing. Any time you feel absolutely certain of something, that's a sure sign that you have missed something. It's sometimes convenient to deliberately ignore something for a while, but if you're absolutely certain, you'll probably miss it forever.

It's easy for certainty to sneak up on you. Even people who are uncertain are usually *certain* about that, too. Either they're sure they're sure, or they're sure they're unsure. Rarely do you find someone who is uncertain about his doubt or uncertain about his certainty. You can create that experience, but you don't usually encounter it. You can ask someone, "Are you sure enough to be unsure?" That's a stupid question, but he won't be sure anymore after you ask it.

The third disease is importance, and self-importance is the worst of all. As soon as one thing is "important," then other things aren't. Importance is a great way to justify being mean and destructive, or doing anything else that's unpleasant enough to need justification.

These three diseases are the way most people get stuck. You may decide something is important, but you can't get really serious about it until you're certain that it's important. At that point you stop thinking altogether. The Ayatollah Khomeni is an excellent example—but you can find lots of other examples closer to home.

Once I pulled up in front of the grocery store in a small town I used to live near. A guy came running over and said angrily, "My friend said you flipped me off."

"I don't think so; do you want me to?"

"Let me tell you something—"

I said, "Wait just one minute," and went into the store and shopped.

When I came back out, he was still out there! When I walked up to my car, he was panting with anger. I picked up a bag of groceries and handed it to him, and he took it. I opened the car door, put the other three bags in the car, took the bag from him and got in the car and closed the door. Then I said, "All right, if you insist," flipped the bird at him, and started to drive away.

As I drove away he burst out laughing hysterically, because I simply would not take him seriously.

For most people, "getting stuck" is wanting something and not getting it. Very few people can pause at that point and question their certainty that this thing is seriously important to them. However, there is another kind of being stuck that no one notices: *Not wanting something and not having it.* That is the greatest limitation of all, because you don't even know you're stuck. I'd like you to think about something that you now recognize is very useful or enjoyable or pleasurable. . . .

Now go back to an earlier time in your life, when you didn't even know about that, or you knew about it but it didn't mean anything to you. . . .

You really didn't know what you were missing, did you? You had no idea how you were stuck back there, and you weren't motivated to change it. You were certain that your understanding was an accurate representation of the world. That's when you're *really* stuck. What are you missing now? . . .

Certainty probably impedes human progress more than any other state of mind. However, certainty, like anything else, is a subjective experience that you can change. Pick a fairly detailed memory in which you were absolutely certain that you understood something. You were in a learning experience; perhaps you were being taught. Maybe it was hard, maybe it was easy, but at a certain time you got that "Oooh, yes! I understand!" feeling. Remember it in as much detail as you need. . . .

Now I want you to remember all that *backwards,* just like running a movie backwards. . . .

When you're done, think about whatever it is that you learned or understood. Is it the same as it was a few minutes ago?

Marty: When I played the picture forwards, I went from a state of confusion to "Aha! I understand!" And then when I ran it backwards, I ended up at the place where I was confused.

Yes, that's running it backwards. What is your experience now, when you think about whatever it is that you were certain you understood a few minutes ago?

Marty: Well, I'm back at the confusion state, and yet part of me knows that I still have the understanding that came later. I can't create the same total feeling of confusion that I had the first time. But I'm not as certain, either.

How about the rest of you. Is it the same?

Ben: Well, I learned something new that I don't know that I was aware of at the time, about what happened with me in the experience.

Well, that's interesting, but it's not what I asked about. I want to know if your experience of what you learned is different.

Ben: No, there's no difference.

There's no difference whatsoever? You have to actually stop and think about it. You can't just say, "Oh, it's the same." That's like saying, "I tried to learn to fly, but I couldn't get out to the plane, so it doesn't work." . . .

Ben: Well, it's funny you mentioned flying, because what I remembered was learning the feel of landing on water—the feel of that contact with the water. When I ran it backwards, I moved out of the feeling of it, and to get the airplane to move backwards I had to view it from a distance. And that added a new dimension to the learning of the touching on the water.

It gave you another perspective. Now do you know anything more about landing a plane than you did before?

Ben: Yeah.

What *else* don't you know? Yet? That's quite a lot to get from just running a movie backwards. A lot of people rerun movies forward as a way of learning from experience, but not many run them backward. How about the rest of you. Is your experience the same?

Sally: No. The details changed. What I pay attention to changed. There's a sequence of things ordered differently.

The sequence is ordered differently. Now, is what you learned different?

Sally: Yes.

How is it different? Do you know something that you didn't know before? Or could you do something different now?

Sally: The body of knowledge is not different. What I learned isn't different, but how I feel about it, and how I look at it, is different.

Would that influence your behavior?

Sally: Yes.

Several of you got quite a lot out of just taking a minute to run an experience backwards. How much would you learn if you ran all your experiences backwards? You see, Sally is absolutely right. Running a movie backwards changes the *sequence* of experience. Think of two experiences: 1) being able to do something, and 2) being unable to do the same thing. First sequence them 1-2, first, you can, and then can't, do something. . . . Now sequence them 2-1, first you can't, and then can, do something. . . . Those are pretty different, aren't they?

The experiences in your life happened to you in a certain order. Most of that sequence wasn't planned; it just happened. A lot of your understanding is based on that somewhat random sequence. Since you have only one sequence, you have only one set of understandings, and that will limit you. If the same events had happened to you in a different order, your understandings would be very different, and you would respond very differently.

You have a whole personal history that's the wealth that you're going to use to go into the future. How you use it will determine what it will produce. If you only have one way of using it, you'll be very limited. There will be a lot of things you won't notice, a lot of places you never go, and a lot of ideas you simply won't have.

Running an experience forwards and backwards are only two of the infinite number of ways that you can sequence an experience. If you divide a movie into only four parts, there are twenty-two other sequences to experience. If you divide it into more parts, the number of sequences is even greater. Each sequence will yield a different meaning, just as different sequences of letters create different words, and different sequences of words create different meanings. A lot of the NLP techniques are simply ways to change the sequence of experiences.

I'd like to install in you what I think is one of the most important steps in the evolution of your consciousness: *be suspicious of success.* Whenever you feel certain, and you succeed at a task several times, I want you to become suspicious of what you're *not noticing.* When you have something that works, that doesn't mean other things wouldn't work, or that there aren't other interesting things to do.

Years ago some people figured out that you could suck creepy gooey black liquid out of the ground and burn it in lamps. Then they figured out how to burn it in a big steel box and roll it all over the place. You can even burn it in the end of a tube and send the tube to the moon. But that doesn't mean there aren't other ways to do those things. A hundred years from now people are going to look at our "high-tech" economy and shake their heads the way we do when we think of ox-carts.

Real innovation would have been easier right at the beginning. They could have done really amazing things. What if they had said "Boy, this really works! What *else* will work? What *else* is there to do? What *other* ways are there to move besides burning stuff and spewing it out the end of something? What other ways are there to move other than rolling in metal boxes and flying in metal tubes?" The more success you have, the more certain you become, and the less likely you are to stop and think, "What is it that I'm not doing?" The things I'm teaching you work, but I want you to think about what else might work even better.

VII

Beyond Belief

Another way to think about behavior is that it's organized around some very durable things called "beliefs." Whenever someone says something is important or unimportant to do, it's because she has a belief about it. You can think about all behavior as being mobilized by the beliefs that we have. For example, you probably wouldn't be learning about NLP if you didn't believe that it would be interesting, or useful, or somehow valuable. Parents wouldn't spend lots of time with their infant children if they didn't believe it would make their children turn out better later on. Parents used to keep young children from getting too much stimulation because they believed it would make them hyperactive; now they give their children lots of stimulation because they believe it will aid their intellectual development.

Beliefs are really phenomenal things. Beliefs can compel perfectly nice people to go out and kill other human beings for an idea, and even feel good about it, too. As long as you can fit a behavior into someone's belief system, you can get him to do anything, or stop him from doing anything. That is what I did with the father who didn't want his daughter to be a whore. As soon as I pointed out that his abusive behavior was exactly the way pimps treat whores, he couldn't do it anymore without violating his own beliefs. I didn't compel him to stop "against his will," whatever that means. I made changing fit into his belief system so completely that he couldn't do anything else.

103

At the same time, beliefs can change. You're not born with them. You all believed things when you were children that you now think are silly. And there are things you believe now that you didn't even think about before . . . taking this workshop, for example.

The word "belief" is a somewhat vague concept to most people, even when they'll gladly go out and kill for one. I'd like to demonstrate what beliefs are made of, and then show you a way of changing them. I'd like someone to come up here who has a belief about *yourself* that you would like to be different. I want you to think of a belief that limits you in some way. Beliefs about yourself are usually more useful to change than beliefs about the world. So pick one that you think would make a real difference to you if it were different.

Lou: I have one.

As if the rest of them don't! Don't tell me what that belief is. I just want you to think of that belief that you'd rather not have. . . . Now set that experience aside for a moment, and think of something you're doubtful about. It might be true, or it might not be; you're really not sure. . . .

Next I want you to tell me how those two experiences of belief and doubt are different. I want you to do the same thing we did earlier with Bill and his understanding and confusion.

Lou: Well, my belief is a big picture. It's bright, vivid and very detailed. Doubt is a much smaller picture. It's dimmer and fuzzier, and it kind of flashes on and off.

OK. Those are pretty clear differences. I can't help noticing that belief is straight ahead of you and doubt is up to your right. Are there any other differences?

Lou: Well, belief nearly fills a big frame and there is very little room for background. Doubt has a lot of background, and there's no frame.

The next step is to take this list of differences and *test one of them at a time,* in order to find out which of them are *most* powerful in changing belief to doubt. For instance, Lou, take the picture of belief, and try making it smaller. . . .

Lou: That makes it seem a little less real, but it doesn't change it very much.

Belief	*Doubt*
large	small
bright and vivid	dim and drab
detailed	fuzzy
stable	flashing
straight ahead	up and right
frame	no frame
little background	lots of background

OK. Bring it back to its original size, and then try removing the frame from around the belief picture, so that you can see more of the surrounding background. . . .

Lou: When I do that, the picture automatically gets smaller, and it's less impressive.

OK. So the frame brings size along with it, and has more impact than size alone. Change it back to the way it was originally, and then change the focus of that belief picture so that it becomes fuzzy. . . .

Lou: That doesn't change it much.

Change that belief picture back again, and then make it dimmer. . . .

Lou: When I do that it starts flashing on and off, a little bit like doubt does.

So changing the brightness also alters the flashing. Change it back again, and then take the belief picture and change its position. Move it from the center of your visual field up to your right. . . .

Lou: That's weird. I feel all kind of floaty, and I can feel my heart speed up. When I start to change the position, all the other things start changing, too. It gets smaller and dimmer and out of focus; the frame fades away and it starts to flash on and off.

OK. Move that picture back to straight ahead of you. The location of the picture changes all other elements, so that is the submodality that is most powerful for Lou in moving something from belief to doubt. But before we do that, we need to have something else to put in its place. Lou, do you know what belief you would like to have in place of the belief you now have?

Lou: Well, I never really thought about that in detail.

Start thinking about it now, and be sure you *think about it in positive terms,* not in terms of negations. Think of what you do want to believe, not what you don't want to believe.

I also want you to frame that belief not in terms of an end or goal, but in terms of a *process* or *ability* that would result in your getting that goal. For instance, if you'd like to believe that you know NLP, change it so that you believe you can pay attention, and learn and respond to feedback in order to learn NLP.

Lou: OK. I know what I'd like to believe.

This new belief is stated in positive terms, without negations, and it has to do with a process leading to a goal rather than the goal itself, right? . . .

Lou: Yes.

Good. Now I want you to do what we call an ecology check. I want you to take a little time to imagine how you would act differently if you already had this new belief, and think of any ways in which this change could be a problem for you, or the people who are close to you, or the people you work with. . . .

Lou: I can't think of any way that it could be a problem.

Good. We'll call that the "new belief." Set it aside for a moment.

Now I want you to take that big picture of the belief you don't like and move it all the way over to where your doubt is. As you do that, the picture will lose its frame and get dimmer, smaller, fuzzier, and start flashing. . . .

Lou: OK. It's over here now, and it looks just like that other doubt picture.

Good. When it flashes off, have that picture of the old belief disappear, and then have the picture of the new belief flash back on. . . .

Lou: OK. The new belief is flashing there now.

Now take that picture of the new belief and move it back to the center of your visual field. As it does this, notice how it develops a frame and gets bigger, brighter, sharper, and more vivid. . . .

Lou: This is incredible! It's right there where the old belief was. I feel like my whole body just got out of prison, and I can feel my cheeks are flushed.

Right. There are a lot of other nice changes going on, too. You can take a minute or two to let those changes settle in, while I respond to a question or two.

Man: Why can't you just take the picture of the desired belief and change it to make it into a belief—the way we made confusion into understanding?

When you made confusion into understanding, there wasn't any other understanding already there to get in the way. You can even have several understandings of the same content without their necessarily conflicting with each other. A belief tends to be much more universal and categorical than an understanding. When you already have a belief, there's no room for a new one unless you weaken the old belief first. Typically the new belief is the opposite of the old belief, or at least very different in some way. Have you ever tried to convince someone of something that is the opposite of what he already believes? Usually the existing belief will prevent him from even considering the new belief. The stronger the belief, the more that will be true.

Think of it this way. Let's say a person believes "X is good," and you succeeded in installing a new belief "X is bad" without changing the old belief. What would you create? . . . What is likely to happen if someone fervently believes in two opposing ideas? . . . One way to deal with that situation is to become a multiple personality. One belief organizes the person in one way for a while; then the other belief takes over and reorganizes the person in a very different way. That's not what I consider a very evolutionary change.

Woman: I want to ask about the "floaty" feeling that Lou reported when you first tried changing the position of the belief picture.

Well, that kind of response tells me two things. One is that I've discovered a submodality change that really makes a profound difference in her experience. The other thing it tells me is that she doesn't yet have a new belief to put in its place. Have you ever had an experience that shattered an old belief, but you didn't have a new belief to put in its place? Some people drift in a haze for days before they can reorganize. That often happens to a person when she gets fired from a job, or a friend or relative dies. I once talked to a man whose college philosophy professor shattered a major belief of his. He said he dropped out and went around in a fog for over six months. I want to have a new belief all "waiting in the wings" before I permanently weaken the old belief.

Now let's come back to Lou, and do a little testing. Lou, is that new belief still there?

Lou: (She looks straight ahead and defocuses her eyes.) Yes. I keep checking to make sure. I have a hard time believing that it could be so easy to do.

What happens when you think of the old belief?

Lou: (She looks up to her left, and then smiles.) It looks kind of dried up now.

It's certainly not where it used to be. This is another way of checking what I've done, and of course I pay more attention to her nonverbal cues that to her words. Now we have a five-minute follow-up. (For information about a videotaped demonstration of this Belief Change Pattern, see Appendix IV.)

I want you all to try out this pattern in groups of three. One of you will be programmer, one will be client, and one will be an observer/consultant. I'll review all the steps again for you before you begin.

Belief Change Pattern

A. *Information gathering and preparation*
1. Belief: "Think of a belief you have about yourself that you wish you didn't have, because it limits you in some way, or has undesirable consequences. How do you represent this belief in your internal experience?"

2. Doubt: "Now think of something that you doubt. It might be true or might not be: you're not sure. How do you represent this doubt in your internal experience?"

When you ask your partner to think of something she doubts, make sure it's something she's unsure of. If she says something like, "I doubt that's a good idea," what she may really mean is that she *believes* it's not a good idea. Doubt is when you waver from thinking something might be true to thinking it might not be true; you just don't know.

3. *Differences:* Do a contrastive analysis to find and list the submodality differences between Belief and Doubt, just as you did before with confusion and understanding.

4. *Testing:* Test each submodality on your list of differences *one at a time* to find out which ones are the most powerful in changing belief to doubt. After testing one submodality, change it back to the way it was originally before testing the next one.

5. *New Belief:* "What new belief would you like to have in place of the belief that you now have and don't like?" Be sure this belief is stated in *positive* terms, without negations. "I can learn to change in response to feedback," rather than "I won't be unable to change what I do."

Also be sure that your partner thinks of the new belief in terms of an *ability* or a *process,* rather than having already achieved a desired goal. "I believe that I can learn to change and maintain my weight" is a useful belief. "I weigh 107 pounds" is not a very useful belief, especially if she actually weighs 350 pounds! We want to mobilize new abilities, not install new delusions.

You also need to ask the person to check for ecology: "If you have this new belief, how could it cause you problems?" "How will your husband or your family respond to you differently if you have this new belief?" "How will this new belief affect your work?" etc. Modify the new belief to take into account any possible difficulties.

Your partner doesn't have to tell you what the new belief is. All you need is a word to identify this new content.

B. *Belief Change Process*

6. *Belief to Doubt:* Keeping the content the same, change the unwanted belief to doubt by using one or more of the most powerful submodalities you discovered in step 4. For instance, if the two most powerful differences were movie to slide, and close panorama to distant framed picture, have the panoramic movie slow to a still slide as it moves away and becomes a framed picture.

7. *Change Content:* Using some *other* submodality, change the content from the old unwanted belief to the new desired belief. Use something she already does, or any gradual analogue method. For example, if she flips pictures back and forth in doubt, she can flip from the old content to the new content. You could have the old belief picture go off into the distance so far that it's impossible to tell what it is, then have it come back with the new belief image. You can have the picture get so bright or so dim that the old content disappears, and then have it come back with the new content, etc.

8. *Doubt to Belief:* Keeping the new content, change doubt to belief by *reversing* the same submodality changes you used in Step 6. If shifting location to the right changed the old belief to doubt, you now shift location back to the left to change the new content from doubt to belief. As you do this, be very alert for any "resistance," or difficulty that your partner has. If the new belief is stated poorly, or has any negations in it, some part of the person may object to it. When you encounter objections, honor them, gather information, and back up to step 5 to redefine the new belief.

C. *Testing*

9. *There are several ways to test.* You can ask "How do you think about this new belief?" Ask for information about submodalites, and use nonverbal behavior to confirm (or disconfirm) the verbal report.

10. When the new belief is in place, the old belief will probably change to the submodalities of disbelief. If you find out how the old belief is represented now, you can compare that with the submodalities of doubt, which you already know, or with the submodalities of disbelief, which you can find out by asking the person to think of something else she firmly disbelieves.

I've often said that good NLP work is 95% information-gathering and 5% intervention. The first five steps are setting things up for the intervention. That makes it easy to make the actual intervention smooth and fast. Remember, brains learn quickly; they don't learn slowly. If you get it all set up ahead of time, it's a lot easier to do a good job. It's a little like setting up a whole string of dominoes, and then tapping the first one.

Go ahead and try this pattern now, in groups of three. I know some of you have questions; many of those questions will be answered by the exercise itself. The questions you still have later will be a lot more interesting after you have had some experience of actually trying out this pattern. My answers will make a lot more sense to you, too.

Now that you've had some experience trying this, let's take some questions and comments.

Man: When I made the belief change, I had a lot of profound internal sensations. It felt as if there were a lot of little fish swimming around in my brain and my body, and the two people observing saw a lot of visible shifts, too. Is this typical?

When the belief is a major one, that's a typical report. Core beliefs organize a lot of a person's behavior. When you make a change in a core belief, you often get a profound internal reorganization. If it's a more peripheral belief, the changes aren't as striking.

Man: I found it hard to think of a useful belief to change. I'd like to hear some content examples of what people changed.

Woman: I've been struggling and struggling for *years* to lose the last five pounds to get to the weight I want to be. It's easy for me to get *close* to the weight I want to be, but I've always believed I had to struggle and fight to control myself in order to lose that last five pounds. So I changed my belief that it was *hard,* to the belief that it will be easy to lose those last five pounds. What a relief; I feel so much more relaxed.

Man: I worked with her on that, and it was really nice to watch her go through the change. Her face, her voice, her whole body—everything was a lot more relaxed afterwards.

Woman: I've had a runny nose and I changed the belief that I couldn't do anything about it. I was amazed, because I can actually feel my nose beginning to dry up.

Man: I started with the belief that it was dangerous for me to drive at night without my glasses. I wanted to change it to the belief that I could safely drive without my glasses at night. Then my partner pointed out that my desired belief was a goal, and that it might be dangerous to change to that belief. I might go driving at night *thinking* I was safe when I wasn't. So we changed to the belief that I *can learn* to drive safely at night without glasses. I think I was really working on a much more general belief that I couldn't learn, *period.* I have a sense that this will affect much more than just driving at night; it seems much broader than that.

Great. Changing the belief that you can't learn something is useful for a lot of people. Many people try something once, don't succeed at it, and conclude they can't do it and they can't learn to do it. I know a man who "knew" he couldn't play the piano: "I sat down at the piano and tried it once, but nothing came of it." I start off with the belief that as long as you have most of your brain cells intact, anyone can do anything. You may need to chunk down the task, or learn to do it *differently,* and it may take you a while to get good at it, but starting with the belief that you can learn will take you a long way. My belief may even be wrong sometimes, but it makes it possible for me to do things and get results that I would never even consider if I assumed people were genetically incapable.

Man: Several people are using firewalking as a way to change people's limiting beliefs. Can you comment on that?

If someone believes they can't do something like firewalking and you get them to discover that it's possible, that can certainly shatter an old belief, particularly if they're told, "If you can walk on fire, you can do anything!" However, there's no way to carefully specify the new belief that gets put in its place. I read about one person who went through a firewalk and said, "Now I believe that I could be standing right at the explosion of a nuclear warhead, and it wouldn't affect me." If he's lucky, he won't ever get to test that belief, but it's an example of the kind of junky beliefs that can get installed that way. If you install beliefs that way, people often put in beliefs that don't relate to evidence or feedback. One firewalk teacher is calling himself "the foremost NLP trainer," when he hasn't even been certified as a master practitioner, much less a trainer! Some of his other beliefs have even less evidence for them.

I know that some people have gotten some very useful belief changes from doing the firewalk. Even a stopped clock is right twice a day. The problem with firewalking is that you have little control over the new belief that takes the place of the old one. There are enough bizarre and dangerous beliefs in the world without adding to them with a random process.

Another problem with something like firewalking is that it tends to install the belief that it takes a really dramatic external event to get you to change. I'd rather install the belief that *change happens constantly, and easily, and making it work for you is a matter of understanding how to run your own brain.* It doesn't take walking on hot coals to do that.

There is a completely separate issue of whether firewalking is actually something that's difficult to do or not, and whether the six hours of evangelistic preparation makes any difference in being able to walk on the coals. A reporter from the *Rolling Stone* timed people as they walked across and found a range of 1.5 seconds to 1.9 seconds, with an average of about 1.7 seconds. The length of the walk was about 10 feet, so if you have a 30″ stride you can easily make it across in 4 steps—two on each foot. That gives a maximum of less than half a second of actual contact per footstep. Firewalkers make a big deal about the temperature of the coals—1,400 to 2,000 degrees—but they don't mention that each foot has only two contacts with the coals lasting less than half a second each. When you pick up a hot coal that's landed on your carpet to throw it back into the fireplace, your fingers probably contact the coal for about that long—and your fingertips are much more sensitive than your feet.

Burning requires heat *transfer*, not just temperature, and the contact time is only one factor in heat transfer. Another factor is conductivity. Let's say you're in a cabin in the mountains and you get out of bed in the morning when it's 20 degrees below zero, and one bare foot lands on a steel plate, while the other lands on a sheepskin rug. Even though the rug and the steel are both at 20 degrees below, the steel will feel a lot colder than the rug, because of it's greater heat conductivity. The conductivity of charcoal is greater than sheepskin, but a lot less than steel. Ask the next firewalker you meet if he's willing to walk the same length on a steel plate that's at the same temperature as those coals!

There is an additional factor that physicists call the "Leidenfrost effect." When there is a significant temperature difference between two substances, and the cooler one is a liquid or contains liquid, a thin vapor layer forms to create an insulating barrier that reduces heat transfer significantly.

All the evidence I have indicates that a ten foot, 1.5 second firewalk is something *anyone* can do, with or without evangelistic preparation, but very few people *think* they can do.

Woman: Some people have beliefs that don't seem to influence their behavior much. For instance, I have a boss who always talks about how people should be nice to each other, but he's usually mean to people himself. How do you explain that?

I try to understand how things work, not "explain" them. There are several possibilities. One is that this belief is not really something he believes, even though he talks about it. A lot of "intellectuals" have beliefs like that which have no effect on their behavior. In that case you could use the belief change pattern to make his belief into one that is subjectively real enough to affect his behavior.

Another possibility is that his belief is real enough, but it's selective: *other* people should be nice to *him*, but he doesn't need to be nice to them, because he's special. Kings, dictators, and some movie stars are like that. Beliefs aren't always reciprocal.

A third possibility is that your boss' belief is real, and reciprocal, but what he thinks of as "being nice" seems "mean" to you. In the 60's a lot of humanistic psychologists would hug everyone too hard because they believed it was a nice thing to do, without noticing whether the "huggee" liked it or not. They'd also go around insulting people, because they thought it was always good to be honest and tell the truth. The crusaders believed that saving souls was an important thing to do, and they didn't care if it was sometimes necessary to kill the body in order to do it.

The process of changing a belief is relatively easy, as long as you have the person's consent. It's a little tougher if the person doesn't want to change a belief. I've also presupposed that you can identify a belief that's worth changing. Sometimes that's not obvious, and it may take some work to determine what someone's limiting belief is. Often the belief that the person *wants* to change isn't the one that actually limits his behavior.

My principal goal here is to teach you a *process* that you can use to change a belief. However, the content that you put into a belief is also important. That's why I asked you to be sure to do an ecology check, as well as to state the new belief in terms of a process, rather than a goal, and to state it in positive terms. I asked you to do this belief change process without knowing the content of the new belief, because I know that some of you would get lost in the content and have trouble learning the process. After you have learned the process thoroughly, you won't be as likely to get lost in the content. When you're working with your clients, it's a good idea to know something about the content, so that you can verify that the new belief is stated in positive terms, is a process rather than a goal, and that it's likely to be ecological. Beliefs are very powerful things; when you change one it can do a lot of good, but if you install the wrong one, it can do a lot of harm, too. I want you to be *very* careful about the kinds of new beliefs you go around installing in people.

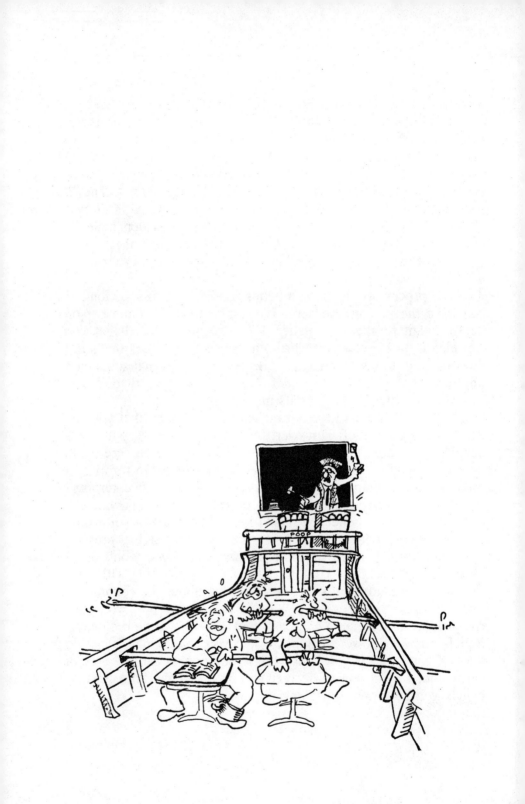

VIII
Learning

I have always thought it was interesting that when people are arguing about a point that doesn't matter, they say "It's academic." John Grinder and I were forced to leave teaching at the University of California because we were teaching undergraduates to do things in their lives. That was the complaint against us. They said school was only for teaching people *about* things.

When I was an undergraduate, the only courses I did badly in were psychology and public speaking. I flunked psychology 1A, and I got a "D" in public speaking! How's that for a joke? NLP is my revenge.

In my contacts with educators, I've noticed that the people who teach a subject may be very good at it, and know a lot about that particular area. However, they usually know very little about *how* they learned it, and even less about how to teach it to someone else. I went to a lecture in a beginning chemistry class once. The professor walked up in front of 350 people and said, "Now I want you to imagine a mirror here, and in front of the mirror is a DNA helix molecule, rotating backwards." Some people in the room were going "Ahhh!" They became chemists. Some people in the room were going "Huh?" They did not become chemists. Some people in the room were going "Urghh!" They became therapists!

That professor had no idea that most people can't visualize in the detailed way that he did. That kind of visualization is a

117

prerequisite for a successful career in chemistry, and it is a skill that can be taught to people who don't yet know how to visualize well. But since that professor presupposed that everyone else could already do what he did, he was wasting his time with most of the people in his classes.

Most studies of the learning process have been "objective." What NLP does is to explore the *subjective* experience of the processes by which people learn things. "Objective" studies usually study people who have the problem; NLP studies the subjective experience of people who have the *solution*. If you study dyslexia, you'll learn a lot about dyslexia. But if you want to teach kids how to read, it makes sense to study people who can read well.

When we made up the name "Neuro-Linguistic Programming," a lot of people said, "It sounds like 'mind control,'" as if that were something bad. I said "Yes, of course." If you don't begin to control and use your own brain, then you have to just leave it to chance. That is sort of what our educational system is like. They keep the content in front of you for twelve years; if you learn it, then they taught it to you. There are a lot of ways that the existing educational system is failing, and I'd like to discuss several of them.

"School phobias"

One of the most pervasive problems is that a lot of kids have already had bad experiences in school. Because of this, a certain subject, or school in general, becomes a cue that triggers bad memories that make a kid feel bad. And in case you haven't noticed, people don't learn very much when they're feeling bad. If a kid's response is really strong, psychologists even describe it as a "school phobia." Feeling bad in response to school situations can be changed rapidly by using a number of the techniques we've described and demonstrated earlier, but I'd like to show you another very simple way to do it.

How many of you have bad feelings about mathematics —fractions, square roots, quadratic equations and stuff like that? (He writes a long string of equations on the board and a number of people groan or sigh.)

Now close your eyes and think of an experience you had that was *absolutely marvelous*—some situation in which you felt excited and curious. . . .

Now open your eyes for a second or two to look at these equations, and then close your eyes and return to that marvelous experience. . . .

Now open your eyes to look at the equations for several seconds more, and then return to your exciting experience again. Alternate a few more times until those two experiences are thoroughly integrated. . . .

Now it's time to test. First look away and think of any experience that's neutral for you, . . . and then look up here at the equations, and notice your response.

Man: My God, it works!

This is actually an old NLP method we call "integrating anchors." If you want to know more about that, you can read *Frogs into Princes.* Changing most bad responses to school can be done that easily and quickly, but you have to know how the brain works to be able to do it. (If you want to try this method yourself, you will find a page of equations in Appendix VI.)

A more imaginative way to use the same principle is to always connect learning with fun and enjoyment to start with. In most schools they have the kids all lined up sitting still in neat, silent rows. I always ask, "How long until the kids get to laugh, move, and enjoy themselves?" If you connect boredom and discomfort with learning, it's no wonder nobody wants to do it. One of the great things about computer-assisted education is that computers are more fun to be with than most teachers. Computers have infinite patience, and never make kids feel bad the way a lot of teachers do.

Remembering

Another major problem for many kids is remembering the stuff they learn in school. A lot of what is called education is simply memorizing. This is changing somewhat. Teachers are starting to realize that the amount of information is so huge, expanding so rapidly, and changing so fast, that memorization isn't nearly as important as they used to think. It's much more important now to be able to find the facts when you need them, use them, and forget them. However, you do have to be able to remember how to do that.

One aspect of memory is similar to what we just discussed: Is the memory paired with a pleasant or unpleasant experience? In order for someone to remember something, he has to go back into the state of consciousness in which the information was provided. That's how memory works. If you make someone angry or unhappy when you ask him to do something, in order to remember it he has to get back into that state. Since he doesn't want to feel bad, he is not likely to remember it. This is why most of us have total amnesia for 12 or 16 years of education. I can't even remember teachers' names let alone most of what I was taught or any of the events. But I can remember the last day of school!

What's your name?

Woman: Lydia.

You forgot your name tag. The only way I can remember names is to hallucinate name tags on people. Every time I meet people I keep looking at their left breast; people think I'm a pervert now. I taught for Xerox once and since everybody had Xerox labels on, I kept calling people "Xerox" all day. It's one of those things; your brain learns to do it, and once it realizes it's of no value it continues anyway.

Lydia, if you forget your name tag, I'll think that you are sneaking into this seminar, and I'll install certain suggestions . . . that will stay with you for the rest of your life. If you have a name tag, I don't do that. You only get suggestions that stay with you for a short period of time.

Lydia, I'm going to tell you a number: 357. Now I want you to forget the number I just told you. . . . Have you forgotten it yet? (No.) If you can't forget one number when a number has no meaning, how could you forget your name tag, or important content in a seminar? Have you forgotten it yet? (No.) Now, how is it possible that you can't forget something that has no importance?

Lydia: If we keep talking about it, I'll remember it even

more. It doesn't matter if it is important or not. Especially since you are asking me to forget it, I won't forget it.

That makes sense. . . . Did you see how many people nodded when you said that? "Oh yeah, you asked me to forget it, so I have to remember it. After all, it has no importance but we are talking about it. If you ask me to forget something that has been talked about for a long time that isn't important, I have to remember it." It's bizarre, isn't it? . . . But she *is* right.

It sounds weird, but even though it sounds weird, you know she's right. Her saying that is as weird as her doing it. Yet psychologists will ignore that as if it has no significance, and go on to study things like "oedipal complexes" and many other strange things. Psychologists will pass up studying how people remember things in favor of studying what "depth" of trance you have been in—that's the metaphor where trance is a hole that you fall into, and going deeper is of great value. The people who talk about "levels of consciousness" disagree; they think it's better to go higher, not deeper.

If I didn't talk about it very long, and talked about it in just the right way, she could forget a number with only three digits. Lydia can forget her name tag, even though people told her it was important. Many of you try to get people to remember things. How many of you talk to people about things that are important, yet they forget what you said? And you thought it was *their* fault! Remember that when you want someone else to remember something.

Except for torturing rats, probably more psychologists' time has gone into studying memory than any other subject. However, they've never really gotten at *how* people do it in terms of subjective experience.

How many of you have trouble remembering telephone numbers? Most of you probably try to do it auditorily, by verbally repeating the numbers to yourself. Many of you were taught the multiplication tables by auditory recitation. Even when that is successful, it's very slow, because you have to recite all those words inside to get to the answer. "Nine, seven, three . . . zero, four, six, eight"; "Nine times six is fifty-four." For a lot of information it's *much* more efficient to memorize it *visually* instead of auditorily: 973-0468, 9 × 6 = 54. When you remember visually, the entire picture pops into your mind at once, and you just skip to the information you need, and read it or copy it down. A lot of kids who are considered "slow learners" are simply remembering auditorily instead of visually. When you take an hour or two to teach them how to do it visually, they learn much more rapidly.

On the other hand, some people try to remember music by making pictures or having feelings, instead of hearing the sounds. So it's always a matter of remembering in a way that's appropriate to what you want to remember.

Another good way to have a bad memory is to do something totally irrelevant to memorizing the data. If you repeat to yourself, "I've *got* to remember the phone number," then what you will remember is that sentence, rather than the phone number! A lot of people do something like that, and then wonder why they have such "bad memories." Actually their memories are excellent; they're just using them to remember idiotic things.

If you study people who have phenomenal memories, you find out that they do some really interesting things. One man with an excellent memory puts subtitles under all his pictures. He actually prints words on his pictures that describe what the pictures are about. That short verbal description codes and categorizes the memory, so that it's easy to go back to it. It's like putting a title on a movie, so you can glance at the title and know what it's about without having to watch the entire movie. In the computer business we call that a "drop tag code"—something that is arbitrary but distinctive, that relates to this and also relates to that, linking them together.

We had a woman in a seminar once who was rapidly introduced to forty-five people by first and last name. That's all it took for her to know everyone's name. I've seen Harry Lorayne do the same thing with about three hundred people on a TV show. When this woman was introduced to someone, she would focus on something very distinctive in what she saw—the shape of the nose, skin coloring, chin, or whatever she spontaneously noticed that was unique about that person. She would continue to focus on this distinctive feature as she heard the person's name, and that would connect the two together. She even checked herself quickly by looking away briefly to visualize that unique feature, and listen for the name, to make sure the connection had been made. I like to have people wear name tags, so I don't have to bother to do that. However, it certainly is a useful talent that could be taught to salespeople. They often have to deal with many people, and it's considered important to remember their names and be personally friendly with them.

If you deal with people mostly over the telephone, this visual method won't work. However, you can easily adapt it to the auditory system: notice something distinctive about the person's voice tone or tempo as you hear the name, and hear the name spoken with that distinctive feature. Very visual people might prefer to imagine the name visually as they hear it. You can always adapt a memory strategy in this way, to make it appropriate to the context or the skills of the person who wants to recall something.

If you *really* want to remember a name, pair it with something unique in all three major representational systems: auditory, visual, and kinesthetic. While you listen to the sound of the name, spoken in his voice tone, you could notice something unique in what you see as you look at him, and also what you feel as you shake hands. Since that gives you a drop tag code in each major system, you will have three different ways to recall the name.

Another way to have a "good memory" is to be as efficient and economical as possible in what you *do* remember, and to use what you have *already* remembered as much as possible. For instance, if you always put your keys in the right front pocket of your pants, you only have to remember that *once*. Someone who puts her keys in many different places may have to remember it four or five times each day, instead of once in a lifetime.

One of our students has a couple of businesses and has to file a lot of papers and records. Whenever something has to be filed, he asks himself, "Where would I look for this when I need it," and starts moving toward the file cabinet. As he does this, an image of a particular file tab appears in his mind, and he files it there. This method uses what he has *already* remembered to organize his files, so he seldom has to remember anything new. Each time he files this item he strengthens the existing connection between it and the file tab, making the system more dependable each time.

One way of thinking about these two examples is that they create a situation in which you have to remember as little as possible. Here's another example. Take a look at the set of numbers below for a few moments, and then look away and see how much of it you can remember. . . .

149162536496481100

Now look at it long enough so that you can still remember it when you look away. . . .

If you have actually tried this, you probably started to group the numbers into twos or threes to organize the task and make remembering easier:

14,91,62,53,64,96,48,11,00
or
149,162,536,496,481,100

This is a process we call "chunking": breaking a large task down into smaller, more manageable, pieces. In business there's an old joke, "How do you eat an elephant?" The answer is, "One bite at a time."

At this point, how long do you think you could remember this number accurately?—an hour?—a day?—a week?

Now let's chunk the number a little differently. Does this suggest anything to you?

1 4 9 16 25 36 49 64 81 100

We can write this same set of numbers a little differently, as *squares* of numbers:

$$1^2 \; 2^2 \; 3^2 \; 4^2 \; 5^2 \; 6^2 \; 7^2 \; 8^2 \; 9^2 \; 10^2$$

Now it's obvious that the number we started with is the squares of the numbers 1 through 10, strung together. Knowing this, you can easily remember this number ten or twenty years from now. What makes it so easy? You have much *less* to remember, *and* it's all coded in terms of things that you have *already* remembered. This is what math and science is all about—coding the world efficiently and elegantly, so that you have fewer things to remember, leaving your brain free to do other things that are more fun and interesting.

Those are just a few of the principles that can make remembering a lot easier and faster. Unfortunately they're not yet used much in mainstream education.

"Learning Disabilities"

One of the nice things that happens after you write enough books is that people let you do things that you wanted to do before, but couldn't. Typically by that time you can't quite remember what they were, but I had written some of them down. When I was asked to work for a school district, I had a few things I wanted to go after. One of them is the whole notion of "learning disabilities," "minimal brain dysfunction," "dyslexia," or "educational handicaps." Those are very important-sounding words, but what they all describe is that *the teaching isn't working*.

Whenever a kid isn't learning, experts are quick to conclude that the problem is a "learning disability," . . . but they're never quite clear about *who has it*! Perhaps you've noticed that they *never* call it a "*teaching* disability." The implication is always that the cause of the failure is that the kid's brain is weak or damaged, often by presumed genetic causes. When people don't know how to change something, they often start searching for a way to justify failure, rather than thinking about how they could try doing something different to make it work. If you assume that a kid has a limp learning lobe, then there's nothing you can do about it until they perfect brain grafts.

I'd rather not explain failure that way. I'd rather think about it as a "*teaching* dysfunction," and at least leave open the possibility that we can learn to change it. If we pretend that you can teach anyone anything, we'll find out where it's not (yet) true. But if we think that when someone isn't learning it means they can't be taught, no one will even try.

In the last century it was common knowledge that man couldn't fly. Then when airplanes became a part of everyday life, most people didn't think it was possible to put a man on the moon. If you take the attitude that anything is possible, you'll find that a lot of things that were previously thought impossible actually do become possible.

The whole idea of "learning disabilities" is based primarily on old neurological "ablation" studies that resulted from a fairly primitive idea of how the brain works: that you can figure out what something does by noticing what happens when it's broken. They would find damage in one part of the brain of someone who couldn't talk, and say, "That's where speech is." That is the same logic as cutting a wire in a television set, noticing that the picture tilts, and saying, "That wire is where the picture straightness is." There are thousands of wires, connections, and transistors involved in holding the picture straight, in a very complex and interdependent system, *and* the brain is a *lot* more complex than a TV set. For some of the more primitive areas of the brain there actually is a certain degree of localization of function. However, it's also been known for years that a young child can lose an entire cerebral hemisphere and learn everything all over again perfectly on the other side.

Recent evidence is throwing out a lot of old neurological dogma. In an X-Ray Tomography study they found a college graduate with an IQ of 120 who had such enlarged brain ventricles that his cortex was only about a centimeter thick! Most of his skull was filled with fluid, and according to dogma, he shouldn't have been able to get up in the morning, let alone go to college!

Another old dogma is that in vertebrates *no* new neurons are formed after birth. Last year they found that the number of neurons in the part of a male canary's brain devoted to singing doubles each spring, and then half of them die off during the rest of the year.

In another study they found that if you remove a monkey's finger, the part of the brain that used to serve the missing finger gets used by the neighboring fingers within a few weeks, and this makes the remaining fingers more sensitive than before. All recent information points to the brain being *much* more flexible and adaptive than we used to think it was.

I never liked the idea of children being "educationally handicapped," because I never thought that reading was primarily genetic. A child can learn to talk in three years, even in the jungle without Ph.D. parents! Why should it take ten more years to teach him to *read* the same thing he already knows how to *say*? Kids in ghettos can learn three languages at once, and they can learn to write all kinds of things in secret codes. But the way things are taught in schools produces a situation in which some kids aren't learning to read. Some of you may remember classes where you didn't learn much because of the atrocious way the material was presented.

Learning to read is really not that difficult. All you have to do is connect the picture of the word with the sound of the word that you already know. If you know the spoken word, you have already connected that sound with an experience of what that word means. When you were a child, you probably learned pretty early that the sound "cat" meant a soft furry little moving thing with claws that meows. The way you do that in your brain is to hear the word "cat" at the same time that you recall your experience of the sight, sound, and feeling of a cat. Then if someone says the word, that experience is there in your mind, and if you see, hear, or feel a cat, the sound of the word is there. All reading does is to add a picture of the word into what you already know. When you see the word "dog," you get a different sound and picture in your mind than when you see the word "cat."

Now that seems pretty simple, and it is. Yet there is an enormous amount of claptrap written about reading problems, and a huge amount of effort goes into trying to solve reading problems. In contrast, there is an NLP-trained group in Denver (see Appendix V) that works with all kinds of educational problems. They will guarantee to raise a kid's reading level, as measured by standard tests, by a *minimum* of one grade level in a set of eight one-hour sessions. Usually they can make much more progress in a shorter time. In the last three years they have only had to pay off on their guarantee once. Their *only* prerequisite is that the kid has muscular stability in using his eyes, so he can see what he's trying to read.

Drugs

One of the other things I wanted to go after in the school

system is the widespread practice of prescribing drugs like Ritalin for "hyperactive" kids who have trouble sitting quietly in rows for long periods of time. Ritalin slows them down so the teacher can keep up with them. Giving these kids drugs is always defended by saying that the drugs are harmless. One of the interesting things about Ritalin is that although it slows down hyperactive kids, its effect on adults is more like an amphetamine: it speeds them up.

So when I talked to this school district I said, "This Ritalin that you're giving the kids slows them down, but it speeds up adults, right? And you're all convinced that it's perfectly safe, and has no harmful side effects, right? Good. I have a proposal that will save you a lot of money. Stop giving it to the kids, and give it to the teachers, so that they can speed up and keep up with the kids." They were boxed in with their own logic, but they still didn't like it. Try suggesting that at your school and find out how many of those "learning disabled teachers" are willing to take a "perfectly harmless drug." The same thing happens with psychiatrists: they almost never prescribe psychoactive drugs for other psychiatrists when they're hospitalized! After thirty years of prescribing phenothiazine drugs, now they've found it causes something called "Tardive Dyskinesia" later in life. It affects your muscles so you shake all over and have trouble walking or picking up a teacup.

Woman: I'm a teacher, and just last week I was in a staff conference with a diagnostician, a nurse, and another teacher. The nurse said, "I think we should prescribe drugs for this kid," and the others nodded their heads. I got really angry, and said, "I can't believe that with all the focus on drug abuse you're recommending that this kid take drugs! How would you like to take drugs?" The diagnostician said, "I take drugs every night to calm down." And the other teacher said, "So do I." And the nurse said, "I take Valium every day." I couldn't believe it, and I was so shocked I didn't know what to say.

Well, taking drugs yourself is a lot different than forcing them on someone else. I think people should choose their own drugs. What's really sad is that most of the problems people are prescribing drugs for can be changed so easily using NLP. Any NLP practitioner should be able to fix a school phobia in half an hour, and most bad spellers can be made into good spellers in an hour or two.

However, you have to be a little careful now. NLP is starting to get well known, and a lot of unqualified people are claiming to have NLP training. There are even a few people claiming to be "the foremost NLP trainer" who have only gone through one training! That's the kind of thing that happens whenever something effective starts to get known, so be a little cautious and ask a few questions of anybody who claims to be trained in NLP.

Some good NLP people are going back into special education classes and wantonly wiping out all kinds of learning problems right and left. When you know how to find out how someone's brain works, it's relatively easy to teach him how to use it in a way that's more effective and efficient.

The capacity for learning is really actualized not when somebody inundates you with the content, but when someone can teach you the mechanism by which it can be done: the subjective structures and sequences that are necessary for learning.

IX

The Swish

The next submodality pattern I want to teach you can be used for almost anything. It's a very generative pattern that programs your brain to go in a new direction. In order to make the pattern easy for you to learn, I'm going to start with something really simple and easy. A lot of people are interested in something called "habit control." Who in here bites his nails and would like not to? (Jack steps up to the platform.) I'm going to use this pattern to get Jack to do something else instead of bite his nails.

What do you see just before you bite your nails?

Jack: I don't know. I don't usually realize I'm doing it until I've done it for a while.

That's true of most habits. You're on "automatic pilot," and later on, when it's too late to do anything about it, you notice it and feel bad. Do you know when or where you typically bite your nails?

Jack: It's usually when I'm reading a book or watching a movie.

OK. I want you to imagine that you're watching a movie, and actually bring one of your hands up as if you were going to bite your nails. I want you to notice what you see as your hand comes up, knowing that you're about to bite your nails.

Jack: OK. I can see what my hand looks like as it comes up.

Good. We'll use that picture in a few minutes, but just set it aside for now. We need to get another picture first. Jack, if you no longer bit your nails, how would you see yourself as being different? I don't mean just that you would see yourself with longer fingernails. What would be the value of changing this habit? What difference would it make to you as a person? What would it mean about you? I don't want you to tell me the answers; I want you to answer by creating a picture of the you that you would be if you no longer had this habit.

Jack: OK. I've got it.

Now I want you to get that first picture of your hand coming up, and make it big and bright, . . . and in the lower right corner of that picture put a small, dark image of how you would see yourself differently if you no longer had this habit. . . .

Now I want you to do what I call "the swish." I want you to make the small dark image quickly get bigger and brighter until it covers the old picture of your hand, which will simultaneously get dim and shrink. I want you to do this really fast, in less than a second. As soon as you've "swished" these images, either blank the screen completely, or open your eyes and look around. Then go back inside and do it again, starting with that big bright picture of your hand coming up, and the small dark image of yourself in the corner. Do it a total of five times. Be sure to blank the screen or open your eyes at the end each time you do it. . . .

Now it's time to test. Jack, make that big bright image of your hand coming up and tell me what happens. . . .

Jack: Well, it's hard to hold it there. It fades out, and that other picture comes in.

The swish pattern directionalizes the brain. Human beings have a tendency to avoid unpleasantness and move towards pleasantness. First there is a big bright image of the cue for the behavior that he doesn't like. As that picture fades and shrinks, the unpleasantness diminishes. As the pleasant image gets bigger and brighter, it draws him toward it. It literally sets up a direction for his mind to go: "from here, go there." When you directionalize your mind, your behavior has a very strong tendency to go in the same direction.

Jack, I want you to do something else. Bring your hand up to your mouth the way you did when you bit your nails. (Jack brings his hand up. Just before it reaches his mouth, it stops and then lowers about half an inch.)

Well, what happened?

Jack: I don't know. My hand came up, but then it stopped. I wanted to put my hand down, but I deliberately held it up there, because you asked me to.

This is a behaviorial test. The behavior that used to lead to nail-biting now leads somewhere else. It's just as automatic as what he did before, but it takes him somewhere he likes better.

This will translate out into experience. As that hand comes up and that compulsion begins in you, the feeling itself will literally pull you in the other direction. It will become a new compulsion. It's not really that you get uncompulsed, it's that you get compulsed to be more of who you want to be.

I did this pattern with a chocolate freak who kept saying she wanted to be "free." She didn't want to be compulsed because it didn't fit with the way she saw herself. After she was done, she couldn't hold a picture of chocolates. It just went "poof." Now when she looks at real chocolate, she doesn't have the old response. The direction of her thoughts is toward being attracted to what she wants to be. It's a new compulsion. You could call this pattern "trade compulsions." I said to her, "Now you're really stuck. You're compulsed to not be able to make these pictures," and she said, "I don't care." She doesn't really object to being compulsed; she just wants to be compulsed in her own way. That's really the difference that makes a difference.

The swish pattern has a more powerful effect than any other technique I've used. In a recent seminar there was a woman in the front row moaning and groaning about having tried to quit smoking for eleven years. I changed her in less than *eleven minutes*. I even chose what to put in the little dark corner picture; I'm not what people call a "non-directive clinician." I told her to see an image of herself politely enjoying other people smoking. I wasn't willing to create another evangelist convert. I didn't want her to see herself sneering at smokers and making life miserable for them.

Now I want you all to pair up and try this pattern. First I'll go through the instructions again.

The Swish Pattern

1. *Identify context.* "First identify where you are broken or stuck. Where or when would you like to behave or respond differently than you do now? You could pick something like nail-biting, or you might pick something like getting angry at your husband."

2. *Identify cue picture.* "Now I want you to identify what you actually see in that situation just before you start doing the behavior you don't like. Since many people are on 'automatic pilot' at that time, it may help to actually *do* whatever has to precede the behavior, so you can see what that looks like." This is what I did with Jack. I had him move his hand toward his face and use that image. Since this is the cue for some response that the person doesn't like, there should be at least some unpleasantness associated with this picture. The more unpleasant this is, the better it will work.

3. *Create outcome picture.* "Now create a second image of *how you would see yourself differently if you had already accomplished the desired change.* I want you to keep adjusting this image until you have one that is really attractive to you—one that draws you strongly." As your partner makes this image, I want you to notice her response, to be sure it's something that she really likes and really attracts her. I want her to have a glow on her face that tells you that what she's picturing is really worth going for. If you can't see evidence that it's worth going after as you watch her, don't give it to her.

4. *Swish.* "Now 'swish' these two pictures. Start with seeing that cue picture, big and bright. Then put a small, dark image of the outcome picture in the lower right corner. The small dark image will grow big and bright and cover the first picture, which will get dim and shrink away as fast as you can say 'swish.' Then blank out the screen, or open your eyes. Swish it again a total of five times. Be sure to blank the screen at the end of each swish."

5. *Test.*

    a. "Now picture that first image. . . . What happens?" If the swish has been effective, this will be hard to do. The picture will tend to fade away and be replaced by the second image of yourself as you want to be.

b. Another way to test is behavioral: Find a way to create the cues that are represented in your partner's cue picture. If that picture is of your partner's own behavior, as it was with Jack, ask him to actually do it. If that picture is of someone else offering a chocolate or a cigarette, or yelling, then I want you to *do* that with your partner and observe what she does and how she responds.

If the old behavior is still there when you test, back up and do the swish pattern again. See if you can figure out what you left out, or what else you can do to make this process work. I'm teaching you a very simple version of a much more general pattern. I know that some of you have questions, but I want you to try doing this first before asking them. After you've actually tried it, your questions will be much more interesting. Take about fifteen minutes each. Go ahead.

As I went around the room, I observed many of you succeeding. Let's not talk about that unless you had difficulty and then came up with something interesting that made it work. I want to hear about when it *didn't* work.

Amy: I want to stop smoking. But when we tested, I still have the urge to smoke.

OK. Describe your first picture for me.

Amy: I see myself with a cigarette in my mouth, and—

Stop. It's very important that you *don't* see yourself in that first picture, and that you *do* see yourself in the second picture. That's an essential part of what makes the swish work. The first picture has to be an *associated* image of what you see out of your own eyes as you start to smoke—your hand reaching for a cigarette, for instance. If you see your hand with a cigarette in it, do you feel compulsed to smoke? Or is it seeing the cigarettes? Whatever it is, I want you to make a picture of what you see that fires off that feeling of wanting to smoke; make a picture of whatever *precedes* smoking. It might be reaching for a cigarette, lighting it, bringing it up to your lips, or whatever else you do. Try the process with that picture, and report back.

Man: Which book has this process in it?

None. Why would I teach you something that is already in a book? You're adults; you can read. I have always thought it was really idiotic for someone to write a book and then to go and read it to people at seminars. But a lot of people do exactly that, and some of them make a lot of money, so I guess it has some use.

Woman: In a lot of the earlier NLP techniques you substitute a specific new behavior. But in this one you just see the way you'd be different if you changed.

That's right. That's what makes this pattern so generative. Rather than substituting a specific behavior, you're creating a *direction*. You're using what's often called "self-image," a very powerful motivator, to set that direction.

When I was in Toronto in January, a woman said she had a phobia of worms. Since Toronto is frozen over most of the year, I didn't think that would be too much of a problem, so I said, "Well, why don't you just avoid them?" She said "Well, it just doesn't fit with the way I see myself." That mismatch motivated her very strongly, even though the worm phobia wasn't actually that much of a problem for her. It wasn't even what I call a "flaming phobia." It was an "ahhh!" phobia, rather than an "AAHHGGH!" phobia. She didn't yet have her brain direction-alized appropriately, but that image of herself kept her trying. So of course I asked her "If you made this change, how would you see yourself differently?" The effectiveness of this pattern depends most importantly on getting the answer to that question. This process doesn't get you to an endpoint—it propels you in a particular *direction*. If you saw yourself doing something in particular, you would only program in that one new choice. If you see yourself being a person with different *qualities,* that new person can generate *many* new specific possibilities. Once you set that direction, the person will start generating specific behavior faster than you can believe.

If I had used the standard phobia cure on her, she wouldn't care about worms at all, and wouldn't even notice them. To get somebody to not care about something is too easy, and there is enough of that going on in the world already. If I had built in a specific behavior, like picking up worms, then she'd be able to pick up worms. Neither of those changes are particularly profound in terms of this woman's personal evolution. It seems to me that there are more interesting changes that a human being can make.

When I swished her, I set up a direction so that she is drawn toward that image of herself as more competent, happier, more capable, liking herself better, and most important, *able to believe that she can quickly make changes in the way she wants to.*

Woman: I think I understand that, but I'm trying to fit it in with some of the NLP anchoring techniques I learned earlier. For instance, there's a technique where you make a picture of how you'd like to be, then step into it to get the kinesthetic feelings, and then anchor that state.

Right. That's one of the old techniques. It has its uses, but it also has certain drawbacks. If someone has a really detailed and accurate internal representation, you can create a specific behavior that will work very nicely. But if you just make a picture of what you'd like to be like, and step inside it to feel what it's like to be there, that doesn't necessarily mean that you *are* there with any quality, or that you learned much along the way. It's an excellent way to build self-delusions, and it also doesn't give you anywhere else to go.

A lot of people go to therapists asking to feel more confident, when they're incompetent. That lack of confidence may be accurate feedback about their abilities. If you use anchoring to make someone feel confident, that feeling *may* allow her to do things she actually could do already but wasn't confident enough to try. That will increase her abilities as well. But it may only create *overconfidence*—someone who is still incompetent but doesn't notice it any more! There are plenty of people like that around already, and they're often dangerous to others as well as to themselves. I've been commenting for years about how many people ask a therapist for confidence, and so few ask for *competence.*

You can change somebody so that he believes he's the very best at something he does, when he can't do it very well at all. When a person is good at *acting* confident, he usually convinces lots of other people to trust in abilities that he doesn't have. It never ceases to amaze me how many people think that if an "expert" acts confident, he must know what he is doing. I figure that as long as you are going to have a false sense of security, you might as well develop some competence along the way.

Where's Amy? Did you finish doing the swish with the new picture?

Amy: Yes.

How long did it take you to do that five times?

Amy: Quite a while.

I thought so. I want you to do it again faster. It should only take you a second or two each time. Speed is also a very important element of this pattern. Brains don't learn slowly, they learn fast. I'm not going to let you do the process wrong and then come back later and say, "Oh, it didn't work." Do it now, and I'll watch you. Open your eyes after each swish. . . .

Now make that first picture. What happens? . . .

Amy: It goes away now.

Do you want a cigarette? (He holds out a pack of cigarettes.)

Amy: No thank you.

Is the compulsion there? I don't care if you smoke or not. I want to know if that automatic urge is there or not. A few minutes ago you said you had the urge to smoke.

Amy: I don't feel compelled to smoke right now.

Here. Hold the cigarettes; take one out and hold it between

your fingers. Look at them; fool with them.

When you do change work, don't back away from testing it; *push it*. Events in the world are going to push it, so you may as well do it so you can find out right away. That way you can do something about it. Observing your client's nonverbal responses will give you much more information than the verbal answers to your questions. (Amy smells the cigarettes, and her facial expression shifts quickly.) Oops, there it is again; the smell of the cigarettes brought back the compulsion. You'll have to go back and do the swish again, and add in smell this time. In that first picture, when you see someone offer you a cigarette, you'll smell that cigarette smell. And in that second picture, you'll see yourself satisfied that you can smell cigarettes and not be compulsed. Go back and do it again that way.

This is called being thorough. A mathematician doesn't just get an answer and say, "OK, I'm done." He tests his answers carefully, because if he doesn't, other mathematicians will! That kind of rigor has always been missing from therapy and education. People try something and then do a two-year follow-up study to find out if it worked or not. If you test rigorously, you can find out what a technique works for and what it doesn't work for, and you can find out right away. And where you find out that it doesn't work, you need to try some other technology.

What I've taught you here is a simplified version of a more general swish pattern. Even so, some of you got lost and confused. Another way to be thorough is to swish in all systems to start with. But it's usually much more economical to just do it in the visual system and then test rigorously to find out what else you need to add. Often you don't need to add in anything. Either that person doesn't need it, or she will add it in on her own without realizing it.

Amy, what happens now when you smell a cigarette?

Amy: It's different. It's hard for me to say how it's different. Now when I smell it I want to put it down, instead of smoking it.

Brains don't learn to get results; *they learn to go in directions*. Amy had learned one set of behaviors: "Would you like a cigarette"—"Yes"—light up and puff. Chairs can't learn to do that

It's quite an accomplishment to learn something like that so thoroughly that no one could influence it for years. She has just used that same ability to learn to go somewhere else.

When you start beginning to use your brain to get it to do what you want it to do, you have to rigorously set up the direction you want it to go, and you need to do it ahead of time. Disappointment is not the only thing that requires adequate planning. Everything else does, too. Without adequate planning you become compulsed to do things you don't want to do: to show yourself old memories and feel bad about them, to do things that destroy your body, to yell at people you love, to act like a mouse when you're furious. . . .

All those things can be changed, but not while you're *in* the situation. You can reprogram yourself later, or you can program yourself ahead of time. Brains aren't designed to get results; they learn to go in directions. If you know how the brain works, you can set your own directions. If you don't, then someone else will.

What I've just taught you is what I often do in a one-day or two-day seminar. The "standard" swish pattern is something that somebody can grab hold of and use, and it will work more often than not. But it doesn't demonstrate to me any competent understanding of what the underlying pattern is. If you give anyone a cookbook, he can bake a cake. But if you give a chef a cookbook, he'll come up with a better product. A really fine chef knows things about the chemistry of cooking that guide what he does and how he does it. He knows what the egg whites are doing in there; he know what their function is. To a chef, it isn't just a matter of throwing a bunch of stuff together and whipping it up. He knows that certain things make things gel into a certain consistency, certain things have to be added in a particular order, and certain other ingredients have to do with changing the flavor in one way or another.

The same thing is true when you begin to use the swish pattern. As a first step toward becoming a chef, I want you to try using the swish pattern again, but find out what happens if you change *one* element. Last time we used the submodalities of size, brightness and association/dissociation as the elements that change as one picture swishes to the other.

Two of those elements, size and brightness, are elements that change continuously over a range. Anything that can be changed gradually is called an *analogue* variable. Association/dissociation is what we call a *digital* variable, because it's either one or the other. You are either inside of an experience, or outside of it; you don't gradually go from one to the other. Association/dissociation will always be one element of the swish. The other two analogue elements can be any two elements that have a powerful effect for the person.

This time I want you to keep everything the same, except you'll use *distance* instead of size. The first picture will start out bright and *close*. The second picture will start out dark and *far away*, and then it will quickly come closer as it brightens, while the first picture recedes into the distance and darkens. This is a fairly small change, and to some of you it may not seem different at all, since size and closeness are strongly correlated. But it is a first step toward teaching you how to use the swish pattern in a much more general and flexible way. Take another fifteen minutes to do the swish with distance, instead of size.

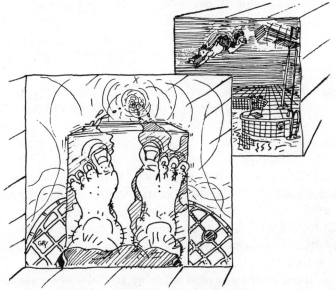

Did using distance rather than size make a difference for some of you? You can use any submodality distinctions to do the swish, but it will only work well if the distinctions you use are subjectively powerful to the person you are working with. Brightness and size are powerful for most people, so the version I taught you first will work more often than not. Distance is another submodality that is important to many people, so I had you try that one next. But if size, brightness, and distance aren't important to the person, then you have to find out which submodalities *are* impactful, and design a swish using those.

A couple of years ago I saw three clients for a videotape session (see Appendix II). The first client I saw was a woman who was suffering from "anticipatory loss." I love the names they come up with to describe how people are messed up! What it boiled down to was that if she had arranged to meet someone who was close to her and that person was a half-hour late, she had what she called a panic attack. She lost her marbles and began to step on them. When I asked her what she would like to have from the session, this is what she said:

> I have a problem with a fear that is almost disabling to me at certain times. When I have it, I sort of go into panic attacks. What I would like to do is distance myself, so that when I'm in the situation I wouldn't experience the fear to the degree that I have it, where I could control myself and make better decisions.

Since she talked about wanting to "distance" herself, she gave me a clear indication that distance was an important submodality for her. She also talked a lot about people who were "close to her" and "close relationships." Later when talking about what she did when someone was late she said, "I need to allow them some distance—I mean allow them some time." With this woman a swish using distance will be much more powerful than one using size. In fact, I went ahead and tried the standard swish using size to find out if it would work. It had very little impact. Then I used distance, and it worked perfectly.

The most important part of doing the swish in a really artistic way is to carefully gather the information you need to set it up appropriately. When someone talks about something being "bigger than life," or being "blown out of proportion," that's a pretty good indication that size is an important variable to use.

When somebody describes a limitation he wants to change, you need to be able to pay attention to how this particular problem works. I always keep in mind that anything that anybody has done is an achievement, no matter how futile or painful it may be. *People aren't broken; they work perfectly!* The important question is, *"How do they work now?"* so that you can help them work perfectly in a way that is more pleasant and useful.

One of the things I do to gather information is to say to the client, "Well, let's say I had to fill in for you for a day. One of the things I would have to do is have your limitation. How would I do it? You have to teach me how to have this problem." As I begin to presuppose that it's an achievement—something learned that can be taught to someone else—it entirely changes the way the person is able to deal with and think about the difficulty.

When I asked the woman who panicked when people were late to teach me how to do it, she said:

> You start telling yourself sentences like, "They're late; they may never come."
> Do you say this in a bored tone of voice—"Ho hum"?
> No. The voice starts out slowly, "Give them another half hour." Then it speeds up as the time gets closer.
> Do you have any pictures in there?
> Yes. I see a picture of the person maybe in a wreck, as if I'm standing there looking on, like through a zoom lens. At other times I'm looking around through my own eyes out at the world and there's no one there.

So in her case she has a voice that speeds up and rises in pitch as time goes on. At a certain point the voice says, "They'll never come" and she makes close-up, zoom-lens pictures of the person in a wreck, or of being all alone.

When I asked her to try making the picture of the wreck, I found that zooming in or out had a very strong effect. When I tested brightness, she said, "The dimness creates distance." That tells me that brightness is also a factor.

Now I want you to pair up with someone and ask him to think of a limitation—something that he considers a problem and wants to change. This time I don't want you to fix it; I only want you to *find out how this achievement works.* Use the frame of "Let's say I had to fill in for you for a day. Teach me what to do." Do the same thing you did earlier when you found out how a person got motivated to do something.

Whenever someone is compulsed to do something he doesn't want to do, something inside has to amplify to a certain point. Something has to get bigger or brighter or louder, or the tone changes, or the tempo speeds up or slows down. I want you to find out how this person achieves this particular limitation. First ask him *when* to do it, and then find out *how* he does it: what does he do on the inside that drives his response? When you think you have identified the crucial submodalities, test by asking your partner to vary them one at a time, and observe how it changes his response. Then ask him to take a different picture and again vary the same submodalities, to see if it changes his response to this other picture in the same way. Find out enough about how it works so that you could do this person's limitation if you wanted to. When you have this information, it will tell you precisely how to swish this particular individual. Don't actually swish them; just gather the information. Take about a half hour.

Man: My partner has two pictures representing two different states: desirable and undesirable. In one of them he sees jerky movement, and in the other one the movements are smooth and graceful.

OK. Do these two pictures create and maintain whatever he considered to be the difficulty? That was my question. I didn't ask about where the person wants to go yet: I only asked how he creates the difficulty. With the woman with panic attacks, she has to get from the state of "Ho, hum" to the state of "freaking out." She starts with a voice and pictures. Then she has to make the voice get faster and higher-pitched, and the picture gets closer and closer as time runs out.

Man: My partner has a feeling of urgency—

Of course. That's the feeling of compulsion. But how does he *make* that feeling? What is the critical submodality? In essence, what you want to know is, "How does this person already swish himself from one state of consciousness to another?"

Man: What makes it different for him is wrapping the picture around him. He pulls it in and around himself and steps into the picture and looks at the picture from his own eyes.

OK. Good. That's how he gets into the state he doesn't want to be in.

Man: Yes. He first gets into that state, and then dissociates by stepping out of it, putting it back over here to his left, away from him, and stands at a distance of several feet away from it.

OK. So association/dissociation is the critical submodality. There aren't that many choices, so we are going to find some repetition. What other critical submodalities did the rest of you find?

Woman: The width of the picture, along with brightness, were critical. When the picture narrowed and dimmed, she felt constrained.

That makes sense. If you get skinny pictures, you feel constrained.

Woman: What she did was like a synesthesia.

These *all* work by synesthesia. That's what we're experimenting with. Think about it. When you change the brightness of an image, it changes the intensity of your feelings. These are all synesthesias. What we want to know is *how* they are related, so we can use that relationship to build a swish.

What you need to know in order to build a swish for her is whether or not narrowing *any* picture makes her response stronger, and whether dimming any picture makes her response stronger. You see, it may be that she uses the word "constrained" because she doesn't like the particular choice that she's left with in that picture. If she sees a choice she likes and the picture narrows, she may describe the feeling as "purposeful," or "committed." If narrowing and dimming make her response stronger, you can build a swish for her by starting with a narrow, dim "problem state" picture which gets wider and brighter as the desired state picture gets narrower and dimmer. That will sound strange to most of you, but keep in mind that everyone's brain is coded somewhat differently. What makes the swish really elegant is designing it so that a particular brain will respond to it strongly.

The other alternative is that making *this* particular picture of few choices narrow increases the intensity her feeling constrained, but that making an image of her with choices gets a stronger response if she broadens it. In that case, you could have the problem picture narrow down to a line, and the solution picture open up out of that same line. So you'll have to go back and find out more about how it works before you'll know the best way to design a swish for her.

I'm telling you about these possibilities so you begin to understand how important it is to tailor your change method to each person. You want to create a direction where the old problem image leads to the solution, and the solution image creates a response of increasing intensity.

Man: My partner had a picture with a double frame—one black and one white—and the image is slanted instead of being straight up and down. The top of the image tilts away from her when she panics.

What changes? Does she bring the image up straight at some time? If the image goes back at an angle and has a border, then she panics?

Man: No, it's just there.

Well, it's not just there. It has to come from somewhere.

What we are looking for here is what *changes*. Once she gets to the picture you described, she has panic. But the image has to start out being somewhat different. I hope she doesn't panic all the time! How does she get there? Does it have to do with the changing of the picture's angle? Or is the angle fixed and something else changes?

Man: It starts out being straight up and down, and as the situation changes, it becomes slanted.

So as the picture tilts, so does she. When it reaches a certain angle, she panics. Does the picture have the double border when it's vertical?

Man: Yes.

So the border is not a critical element, it just happens to be there. Does anything else happen as the picture tilts? Does it change brightness or anything like that? Does the speed of the images change?

Man: No. The sound also becomes sort of blurred and buzzy.

And you are sure that nothing else changes visually.

Man: No.

Good. I'm glad you're not sure. It seems like just tilting an image wouldn't be enough. You can go back and ask her. Have her take a picture of something else and tilt it and find out what happens. If just tilting any picture is enough to make her feel "off-balance" and panic, you could have the first picture tilt down to a line while the second picture tilts up to the vertical. Or you could tilt the first picture down, and then flip it all the way over to show the second picture on the other side. Take her for a real ride! Have you seen the video effects on television in which a square comes out and flips around? As it flips around it ends up being a new image. You could do it that way. Are you all beginning to understand how you can use this information to construct a swish that will be especially powerful for a particular person?

Man: My partner's problem was caused by the fact that he lost the background of what he was looking at. It just began with a lot of people in a background, and when he got to a critical place, the background was all gone; there were just people there.

Was there a change in the focus, or the depth of field?

Man: It just disappeared. I guess it's out of focus. It's not there.

But the things in the foreground are clear?

Man: They are as clear as normal; they are not changed.

Is it like looking through a lens? With a lens you can get one part to be clear and the other parts are blurred. Is that sort of what you are talking about?

Man: No, it isn't. It's as if he put a mask over everything except the people involved, and everything else disappeared.

And the people are standing on nothing?

Man: I guess the chairs and things they were sitting on would be there, but everything else in the room was cleared. The concentration was apparently on people.

OK. But you don't know *how* it was done—with focus or whatever?

Man: No, I don't know that.

That is the part you need to know. You want to know *how* the transition occurs, so that you can use that method of transition with *any* picture.

Woman: The fellow I was working with had a still slide, with no movement or color. When he first sees the picture, he talks in his own voice, and it's a mid-range tone of voice: "Hmmmm, not bad," the tone going down and up. Fairly quickly the voice changes and becomes monotonous and low. That's when he feels bad.

The picture remains constant? It doesn't change at all? I find it a little difficult to believe that while he changes his tone and tempo of speech, the slide remains constant—that the brightness or something else about it doesn't change—because I simply haven't found it. That doesn't mean it's not possible, but I find it very unlikely. People can lead auditorily, but usually something else changes along with the voice. Let's assume that he's looking at a picture and he just talks himself from one state to another by changing his tone of voice. That will work. You will also need another auditory parameter if you are going to do an auditory swish. Probably the tempo will change. There will usually be more than one parameter that changes.

Man: If you are looking for another variable, and could get

one in another modality so you had one visual and one auditory submodality, would that mixture work?

It can, but most of the time you don't need it. You could do that if you really couldn't find a second submodality in the same system. The reason I'm emphasizing the visual system is because the visual system has the property of *simultaneity*. You can easily see two different pictures together at once. The auditory system is more sequential. It's hard to pay attention to two voices at once. You can do a swish auditorily, but you have to go about it a little differently. If you learn to be precise in the visual system, then when you start dealing with the auditory channel it will be easier to adapt.

Man: The reason I asked that is because with my partner the pictures change, but also as she steps into the picture, she can hear herself. I'm wondering in doing the swish whether it would sort of nail it shut by adding an auditory piece.

Yeah. "Nailing it shut" is a good way to think about it. If you do a swish with only one submodality, that's like nailing two boards together from only one direction. A dovetail joint has nails or screws going into it from *two* directions at once. If you pull one way, one set of nails holds it; if you pull the other way, the second set of nails holds it. That's why it's important to use two powerful submodalities simultaneously when you do the swish. People usually won't vary more than one submodality at a time on their own, and you'd have to vary at least two at once to undo a swish.

If you're doing a visual swish and there are also auditory components, typically the person will *demonstrate* the auditory shifts to you unconsciously as she tells you about the two pictures. Then when you are telling her to make the pictures, you can do the auditory shifts externally with your voice, without mentioning it. In order to do that well, you need to be able to speak in someone else's voice.

The skill to be able to copy someone else's voice is simply a matter of practice, and it's a talent that is well worth learning to do in this business. After a while you discover that you don't have to match someone perfectly; you just have to get a few distinct characteristics. You need enough so that if you do some-body's voice, he won't notice whether *he* is talking to himself or *you* are. It's the old pattern of, "Well I went inside and said to yourself . . . " I used to do that a lot in workshops, and very few people noticed.

I want you all to go back to the same person you were with a few minutes ago, and find out the one or two analogue sub-modalities that are most important in creating the limitation. Some of you already have that information, but a lot of you don't.

Next I want you to get that second picture of how he would see himself differently if he no longer had the limitation. This picture must be dissociated, and the first picture will always be associated. Association in the first picture and dissociation in the second will always be one element of the swish.

Next you'll build a swish using the two analogue submodalities you've identified as important (instead of the size and brightness you used in the standard swish). First have your partner make an associated picture of the cues, using whatever submodalities create a strong response (a big, bright picture). Then have your partner make a dissociated picture of themselves as they would like to be, beginning with the other extreme of those same submodalities (a small, dim picture). When you swish, the submodalities will change so as to rapidly weaken the response to the first picture at the same time that they strengthen the response to the second picture. Come back in about half an hour.

What you have been doing is the basis for using the swish artistically and with precision. You can always just try the standard swish. If it doesn't work you can try a different one and keep going until you find one that works. That is certainly better than not trying another one. But it's even better to gather enough information so that you know exactly what you're doing, and you can predict ahead of time what will work and what won't. Do you have any questions?

Man: What do you do with a client who doesn't have much awareness of internal process? When I ask some of my clients how they do things inside, they just shrug and say, "I don't know."

There are several things you can do. One is to keep asking until they pay attention inside. Another is to ask a lot of questions and read the nonverbal "yes/no" responses. Ask, "Are you talking to yourself?" and watch the response just *before* the verbal "I don't know." This technique is discussed fully in the book *Trance-formations*.

Another thing you can do is to create the problem situation and observe the person's behavior. All submodality shifts are demonstrated in external behavior. For instance, when someone brightens a picture, the head rotates back and up, but when a picture comes closer, the head moves straight back. If you observe people when you ask them to make submodality changes, you can calibrate to the behavioral shifts that we call "submodality accessing cues." Then you can use those shifts to determine what someone is doing inside, even when he's not aware of it. I always use this calibration as a check to be sure the client is doing what I ask him to.

Like everything else in NLP, the more you know how change works, and the more you are calibrated to behavioral responses, the more you can do things covertly. For instance, sometimes a person has to practice the swish a few times. You can ask her to do it once, and then ask her, "Did you do it right?" In order to answer that question, she'll have to do it again. Then you can ask, "Are you sure you did it right?" and she'll have to do it again. She'll also do it faster and easier that way because she isn't consciously trying to do it.

Woman: Do you have any long-term follow-up studies of the effectiveness of this method?

I'm much more interested in twenty-minute follow-up studies. The only good reason for a long-term follow-up study is if you can't tell when the person changes in your office. Think about this: if you did produce a change in someone and they remained changed in that way for five years, what does that prove? That says nothing about whether or not that change is a valuable one, or whether or not it could have evolved any further. You see, making it possible for a woman to not be phobic of worms or not be compulsed to eat chocolate, is not a very profound accomplishment, even if it lasts the rest of her life. The important thing to understand about the swish pattern is that it sets the person in a direction that is generative and evolutionary. When I have done longer-term follow-ups on people I've swished, they typically report that the change I had made became the basis for all kinds of *other* changes that they are pleased with. The swish pattern doesn't tell people how to behave, it keeps them on the track of going toward what they want to become. To me, setting that direction is the biggest part of what change is all about.

(For information on videotapes of the Swish pattern, see Appendixes II and IV.)

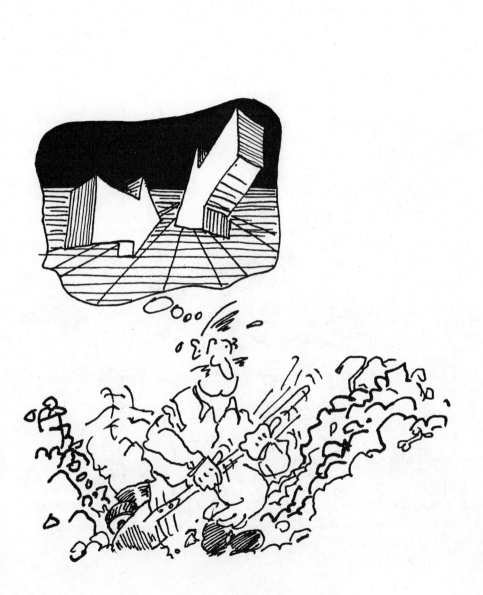

Afterword

There is one thing that more than anything else delineates when somebody knows what NLP is. It is not a set of techniques, it's an attitude. It's an attitude that has to do with curiosity, with wanting to know about things, wanting to be able to influence things, and wanting to be able to influence them in a way that's worthwhile. Anything can be changed. That's something Virginia Satir said the first time I saw her give a workshop, and it's absolutely true. Any physicist knows that. Any human being can be changed with a .45—that's called "co-therapy with Mr. Smith and Mr. Wesson." Whether a change is useful or not is a more interesting question.

The technology that you have been learning here is very powerful. The question about how you will use it, and what you will use it for, is one that I hope you will consider very carefully —not as a burden, but with the curiosity to find out what's *worthwhile*. The experiences in your life which have been the most beneficial to you in the long run, and which provide the basis of your being able to have pleasure, satisfaction, enjoyment, and happiness, were not necessarily utterly enjoyable at the time they occurred. Sometimes some of those experiences were as frustrating as they could be. Sometimes they were confusing. Sometimes they were fun in and of themselves. Those experiences are not mutually exclusive. Keep that in mind when you design and provide experiences for others.

I got on a plane once to go to teach a seminar in Texas. The guy sitting next to me on the plane was reading a book called *The Structure of Magic.* Something about the cover caught my eye. I asked him, "Are you a magician?"

"No, I'm a psychologist."

"Why is a psychologist reading a book about magic?"

"It's not a book about magic, it's a serious book about communication."

"Then why is it called *The Structure of Magic*?"

Then he sat there for three hours and explained to me what the book was about. What he told me about that book had nothing to do with what I thought I was doing when I wrote it. At best the relationship couldn't even have reached being tenuous; he got lost in chapter two. But as he told me about the book, I asked him questions, such as, "How specifically?" and "What, specifically?"

"Well, if you look at it this way . . . "

"If I were to look at it that way, what would I be seeing?"

"Well, you take this picture, you know, and take the other picture (He didn't know that most people don't have two pictures all the time), and you make this picture smaller and this one larger. . . ."

As he began to describe these things that were very matter-of-fact for him, I was sitting there thinking, "Wow, that's weird. There might be a whole new world here!"

He told me that he just happened to be going to Texas to an NLP workshop. When he saw me walk in the door the next day, he was very pleased that I had taken his advice and decided to come to it . . . until I walked up on stage and put on the microphone! What he probably will never appreciate is that the reason I didn't just sit down and say, "I wrote that book," was because I didn't want to deprive myself of the opportunity to learn.

You see, whenever you think that you understand totally, that is the time to go inside and say, "The joke is on me." Because it is in those moments of certainty that you can be sure that the futile learnings have set in, and the fertile ground has not been explored. Obviously there is always a lot more left to learn, and that is the fun part of NLP, and its future.

When you master something so throughly that you can do it perfectly, then it becomes a job, no different than running a staple gun. You could set up a clinic and have people come in and cure phobias, over and over again, all day long. There is no difference between that and any other routine. However, when each of those people comes in, you could also begin to explore how to make it more interesting and more worthwhile than just curing a phobia so that someone isn't terrified of an elevator. Why not make it so someone can *enjoy* riding in elevators? Why not figure out how phobias are done, and give away phobias of something more worthwhile? There are some things worth having a phobia of! Do you have any compulsive spending habits? —violence habits? —eating habits? —consumption habits? How about a phobia of being stagnant and bored? That might propel you into interesting new places.

Whenever I travel to do a seminar, I always arrive at the hotel the night before. When I went to Philadelphia recently, there were a lot of "advanced" neuro-linguistic programmers staying at the same hotel, and most of them had never met me. When I went down to the bar, one of them had just said to a friend, "I hope this isn't just more of that submodality stuff, because I already know that." So of course I walked up and asked, "What the hell is NLP?"—something I wouldn't miss for the world.

"Well, it's hard to explain."

"Well, you do NLP, right? Do you do it well? Do you understand it?"

"Oh, yes, of course I do."

"Well, I'm a simple person. Since you're an expert, can you tell me about this? Go ahead, I'll buy you another drink and you just tell me all about it."

In his wildest fantasies he had no idea the feeling he would have at 9:30 the next morning when I walked onto the stage at the seminar. He also had no idea that he taught me more in the bar than I taught him in the seminar during the next three days.

I'd like you to consider making *everything* into an introductory seminar, in the sense that you never learn so much that you miss what else there is to know. All too often, people forget how to *not* know. They say, "Oh, yeah, that sounds like . . . " "This is the same as . . . " "Yeah, I learned all that submodality stuff last year. . . ." I haven't learned it all yet, so if they learned it all last year I wish they would tell me, so I don't have to work so hard to figure it out!

There is a huge difference between learning some things, and discovering what there is still to learn. That is the difference that makes the difference. There are things I know how to do that they don't even *suspect*. But the reverse is also true. Since everybody has submodalities, everybody does interesting things with them. They may not consciously know how they do them, but still they are able to do and use unique configurations. When clients come in and you ask, "How are you broken?" they'll actually answer that question. But don't forget that they are "broken" so well they can do their problem the same way over and over again! That can always remind you that it's an achievement, no matter how futile, disgusting or repulsive it may be.

The ability to be fascinated by the complexity of that achievement distinguishes somebody who is working in a *generative* way from one who is working in a *remedial* way. Without that sense of curiosity, those things which are futile, repulsive and disgusting will be things that you won't know how to influence. Without that influence, people will continue to fight wars over strange places and over insignificant differences, without being able to find new ways in which everybody can come out ahead. The essence of being generative is to create a world in which everybody gains because there are ways of creating *more,* rather than having a limited amount to fight over and divide up.

Everything a human being can do is an achievement, depending only on where, and when, and for what, it is utilized. Each of both of you can do something about that, because each of both of you is going to drive your own bus. Now that you know *how,* the interesting question is *where*? When you can't drive your bus, it doesn't matter much where you try to go, because you won't get there anyway. When you learn how to use your brain, that question becomes crucially important. Some people drive in circles. Some people take the same route every day. Some people take the same route, but it takes them a month instead of a day.

There is *so* much more inside our minds than we suspect. There is *so* much more outside than we are capable of being curious about. It's only that growing sense of curiosity that allows you to capture the enthusiasm that makes even the most mundane, or the most fascinating task worthwhile, fun, and intriguing. Without that, life is nothing more than waiting in line. You can master the art of tapping your foot while you wait in line, or you can do much more. And I have a surprise for you. I've found out that the after-life begins with a long wait in line. You'd better have some fun now, because those who enjoy themselves and do things that are worth doing with a great sense of curiosity get to stand in a shorter line than those who have only developed the ability to wait in line.

No matter where you are or what you are doing, the skills, the techniques and the tools that you have acquired here serve as the basis for amusing yourself, and for learning something new. That man who flew with me to Texas, and explained to me what NLP was, is only different from me in one way. The next morning when he sat down and looked up and saw me, and thought, "Oh, my God!" he didn't realize that I learned something from him. That is the only difference between me and him. I didn't do it to make a fool out of him; I did it in order to learn, because I was curious. *It was a rare and unprecedented opportunity. And so is every other experience in your life.*

Appendix I
Submodality Distinctions

The list below is not complete, and the order of listing is irrelevant. What distinctions do *you* make internally that you can add to this list?

Visual:

Brightness
Size
Color/black and white
Saturation (vividness)
Hue or color balance
Shape
Location
Distance
Contrast
Clarity
Focus
Duration
Movement (slide/movie)
Speed
Direction
3-Dimensional/flat
Horizontal or vertical hold
Sparkle

Perspective (point of view)
Associated/ dissociated
Foreground/background
Self/context
Frequency or number (split screen or multiple images)
Frame/panorama (lens angle)
Aspect ratio (height to width)
Orientation (tilt, spin, etc)
Density ("graininess," "pixels")
Transparent/opaque
Strobe
Direction of lighting
Symmetry
Digital (printing)
Magnification
Texture

Auditory:

Pitch	Distance
Tempo (speed)	Contrast
Volume	Figure/ground
Rhythm	Clarity
Continuous or interrupted	Number
Timbre or tonality	Symmetry
Digital (words)	Resonance with context
Associated/dissociated	External/internal source
Duration	Monaural/stereo
Location	

Kinesthetic:

Pressure	Movement
Location	Duration
Extent	Intensity
Texture	Shape
Temperature	Frequency (tempo)
Number	

One useful way to subdivide kinesthetic sensations is the following:

1) *Tactile:* the skin senses.

2) *Proprioceptive:* the muscle senses and other internal sensations.

3) *Evaluative meta-feelings* ABOUT other perceptions or representations, also called emotions, feelings, or visceral kinesthetics which are usually represented in the chest and/or abdomen or along the mid-line of the torso. These feelings are not direct sensations/perceptions, but are representations *derived from* other sensations/perceptions.

Olfactory and Gustatory (smell and taste)

The terms used by psychophysics experimenters (sweet, sour, bitter, salt, burnt, aromatic, etc.) probably won't be useful. The fading in or out (changes in intensity and/or duration) of a particular taste or smell that you identify as relevant in someone's experience may be quite useful. Odors and tastes are very powerful anchors for states.

Appendix II
Richard Bandler Client Videotape Sessions

Richard Bandler demonstrates the clinical application of the NLP methods described in this book in three half-hour studio-quality videotape sessions with clients. (Transcripts of these sessions appear in the book *Magic in Action*.)

1. *"Anticipatory loss"* A woman who experienced disabling panic attacks whenever someone close to her was late for an appointment is cured of her problem.

2. *"Authority figures"* A young man is helped to overcome his fear of authority figures.

3. *"Agoraphobia"* A middle-aged truck driver is cured of his 6-year inability to leave the city limits of the town he lives in.

All three tapes include a follow-up session demonstrating the success of the session. Each tape shows the entire unedited session with these clients, none of whom had previously met Richard Bandler. The price of the tapes is $75 each, or $150 for all three tapes (VHS Format only). Make checks payable to: Marshall University Foundation (No postage or handling charges.) Order from:

Dr. Virginia Plumley
Marshall University
Huntington, WV 25701
(304) 523-0080

Appendix III
Richard Bandler Hypnosis Seminar Videotapes

These three 45 minute videotapes were edited from a weekend hypnosis seminar conducted in Florida in 1983.

1) *Induction*. Different induction methods are described and demonstrated, including dissociation, arm levitation, self-hypnosis, and naturally occurring trance states.

2) *Utilization*. Internal states and submodalities are used to change unpleasant memories, and to cure a phobia.

3) *Metaphors for Change*. Richard demonstrates the conversational use of metaphors for changing a person's limiting beliefs, and creating personal change.

Each videotape costs $60.00. The set of three videotapes costs $150.00. Add $1.25 for postage and handling. Specify VHS or Beta format and make check payable to:

Hypnosis Vo-Cal Production
P.O. Box 533
Indian Rocks Beach, FL 33535
(813) 596-2357

Appendix IV
NLP Training Videotapes

These videotapes of NLP Training sessions and/or NLP work with individuals were produced by Connirae and Steve Andreas. The most sophisticated and sensitive VHS format system available was used for the original tapes, which have been professionally edited and duplicated for high quality.

1. *The Fast Phobia/Trauma Cure.* An intense 20-year phobia of bees is eliminated in 6 minutes, using the fast phobia/trauma cure developed by Richard Bandler. An introduction and discussion accompanies the session, and includes an 11-month follow-up interview with the client. Also included is a 15-minute follow-up interview with a Vietnam Veteran whose "post-traumatic stress syndrome" lasting 12 years was completely changed in one session using this method. 42 minutes, $50.

2. *Changing Beliefs.* The belief change pattern developed by Richard Bandler is demonstrated in an Advanced NLP Submodalities Training. An explanation of what is being done accompanies the demonstration, and is followed by questions, discussion, and preparation for a practical exercise using the pattern. A three-month follow-up interview with the client is also included. 104 minutes, $85.

3. *Future-Pacing: Programming Yourself to Remember Later.* How people program themselves to remember something automatically in the future is explored in this session taken from the second day of a 24-day NLP Practitioner Training in January, 1985. 79 minutes, $65.

4. *The Swish Pattern.* The swish pattern is an amazingly rapid, powerful, and generative new submodality intervention developed by Richard Bandler. The first demonstration uses the Standard Swish on a simple habit, nail-biting. The client in the second demonstration went into uncontrolled anger when her daughter spoke in a certain voice tone. This example shows how to test thoroughly to find out precisely which submodalities are powerful for the client, and designing an appropriate swish — in this case in the auditory system. 71 min., $65

All four tapes $225 (this is a 15% reduction). All prices postpaid within the U.S. Other tapes are in preparation; write for a current list. Please send a check with your order specifying VHS or Beta format, to:

NLP of Colorado
1221 Left Hand Canyon Dr., JSR
Boulder, CO 80302
(303) 442-1102

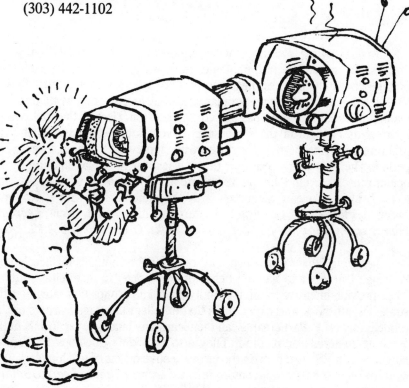

Appendix V
NLP Educational Consultants

New Learning Pathways will guarantee a *minimum* of one year's progress in structural and phonetic analysis, word comprehension and passage comprehension as measured by two widely accepted tests: 1) The Woodcock Reading Mastery Standardized Test, and 2) The Ekwall informal reading inventory for long passage comprehension. Usually they get two or three years change on these measures, given both before and after their program of eight one-hour sessions (with homework) over a seven-week period. The only prerequisite for this is a test for muscular stability of the ocular muscles around the eye, to be sure the child can see what he is trying to read. They also teach seminars for teachers and consult with educational systems. Please call or write for current information. *New Learning Pathways, P.O. Box 5044-142, Thousand Oaks, CA 91359, (805) 492-5024*

Learning How to Learn specializes in NLP techniques for accelerated language learning and gaining behavioral competence in foreign cultures. They provide intensive training to individuals and groups that integrates the strategies, attitudes, and experiences that excellent language learners use, as modeled by NLP. Participants can then learn any language regardless of the teaching materials or method. They also provide workshops for foreign language and ESL teachers on the most effective means of teaching language acquisition in the classroom environment. *Learning How to Learn, 1340 W. Irving Park Rd., Ste 200, Chicago, IL 60613*

Appendix VI

$$\frac{y_1 - y_2}{x_1 - x_2} = \frac{-(y_1 - y_2)}{-(x_1 - x_2)}$$
$$\sqrt[n]{a^n b^{n+1} c^{n-1}}, \; n \in \{3, 5, 7, \ldots\}$$

$$\frac{5^4 - 2^4}{5^2 + 2^2}$$

$$xyz + x^2 yz^3 + x^3 y^2 z + (^-1)xy^3 z^2$$
$$2^3 \cdot x^2 y + 2^5 \cdot x^2 y + 2^3 \cdot x^2 y + 2^5 \cdot xy^2$$
$$3^2 \cdot ab^2 + 3a^2 b + 3^3 \cdot a^2 b^2 + 3^4 \cdot a^2 b^2$$

$$(\forall_x)(\exists!_y)(x + y = 0)$$

$$\frac{(2ab)^2(3ab)}{(-6a^3 b)^2}$$

$$\frac{8hn^3 \qquad + 2n^4}{3hn^3 + hn + \; n^4}$$

$$(3x^2 y)(5x^4 y^3) = 15x^6 y^4$$

$$\frac{5 - 11y + 2y^2}{4y^2 - 9} \cdot \frac{2y + 3}{1 - 2y} \cdot \frac{(5 - y)^{-1}}{2y - 1}$$

$$\frac{(2y^2)^3 (2y)}{(2y)^3 (2y)^2}$$

$$V = \tfrac{4}{3}\pi r^3$$

$$\frac{14x^3 - 21x^2 - 14x}{4x - 16x^3}$$

$$\left(\frac{x^4 - 13x^2 + 36}{2x^2 - 18} \div \frac{x^3 - 2x}{x - 5}\right) \cdot \frac{2}{x - 5}$$

$$\left(\frac{3b - 1}{b - 3}\right)^{-1} \cdot \frac{1 + 3b - 18b^2}{6b^2 - 17b - 3}$$

$$I = \frac{nE}{R + nr}$$

169

Selected Bibliography

Bandler, Richard. *Magic in Action*. 1985 (cloth $14.95)

Bandler, Richard; and Grinder, John. *Frogs into Princes*. 1979 (cloth $10.00, paper $6.50)

Bandler, Richard; and Grinder, John. *Reframing: Neuro-Linguistic Programming and the Transformation of Meaning*. 1982 (cloth $10.00, paper $6.50)

Grinder, John; and Bandler, Richard. *Trance-formations: Neuro-Linguistic Programming and the Structure of Hypnosis*. 1981 (cloth $10.00, paper $6.50)

For information about other NLP books by Richard Bandler and others, write to:

Meta-Publications
P.O. Box 565
Cupertino, CA 95014
(415) 326-6465

(415) 965-0954

(408) 475-8540

Index